GOALWORK

Annual Planning Tool

Wise Work Books

Tools for Transformation, Training, and Development

Fail to Plan, Plan to Fail

Because success is no accident.

Theme

Resolutions

1. _____
2. _____
3. _____
4. _____
5. _____

Time Frame: _____

Draft Goals	Priority Order	Supports Objectives	Simple / Complex	Target Date

Achieved!		Finalized Goals
		1.
		2.
		3.
		4.
		5.
		6.
		7.
		8.
		9
		10.
		11.
		12.
		13.
		14.
		15.
		16.
		17.
		18.
		19.
		20.
		21.
		22.
		23.
		24.
		25.
		26.
		27.
		28.
		29.
		30.

Year _____

First Quarter		
January	**February**	**March**

Second Quarter		
April	**May**	**June**

Year _____

Third Quarter		
July	**August**	**September**

Fourth Quarter		
October	**November**	**December**

Year

First Quarter		
January	February	March

Second Quarter		
April	May	June

Year _____

Third Quarter		
July	August	September

Fourth Quarter		
October	November	December

Simple Goals

Goal # _____

Specific	Measurable	Achievable	Realistic/Relevant	Time-bound

Use positive language to rewrite your finalized goal including the SMART elements from above.

_____

_____

What's your motivation?

_____

_____

Supports objectives: _____

Define this goal.

_____

_____

_____

_____

_____

_____

Success Checklist
Prework
Build SMART Goal
Know Why
Develop Details
Identify Resources
Develop Action Plan
Work
Visualize
Take Action
Achieve Goal!
Postwork
Celebrate
Evaluate

Identify resources and skills available and/or needed.

_____   _____

_____   _____

_____   _____

_____   _____

Action Plan	
Steps To Take	**Timeline**

Reward:

_____

Evaluation notes and lessons learned:

_____

_____

_____

_____

_____

_____

_____

_____

_____

_____

Goal # _____

Specific	Measurable	Achievable	Realistic/Relevant	Time-bound

Use positive language to rewrite your finalized goal including the SMART elements from above.

_____

_____

What's your motivation?

_____

_____

Supports objectives: _____

Define this goal.

_____

_____

_____

_____

_____

_____

Success Checklist
Prework
Build SMART Goal
Know Why
Develop Details
Identify Resources
Develop Action Plan
Work
Visualize
Take Action
Achieve Goal!
Postwork
Celebrate
Evaluate

Identify resources and skills available and/or needed.

_____   _____

_____   _____

_____   _____

_____   _____

Action Plan	
Steps To Take	Timeline

Reward:

_____

Evaluation notes and lessons learned:

_____

_____

_____

_____

_____

_____

_____

_____

_____

_____

_____

□ _____
Date Completed

Goal # _____

_____

Specific	Measurable	Achievable	Realistic/Relevant	Time-bound

Use positive language to rewrite your finalized goal including the SMART elements from above.

_____
_____

What's your motivation?

_____
_____

Supports objectives: _____

Define this goal.

_____
_____
_____
_____
_____
_____

Success Checklist
Prework
Build SMART Goal
Know Why
Develop Details
Identify Resources
Develop Action Plan
Work
Visualize
Take Action
Achieve Goal!
Postwork
Celebrate
Evaluate

Identify resources and skills available and/or needed.

_____   _____
_____   _____
_____   _____
_____   _____

Action Plan	
Steps To Take	**Timeline**

Reward:

_____

Evaluation notes and lessons learned:

_____
_____
_____
_____
_____
_____
_____
_____
_____
_____

15

Goal # _____

_____

Specific	Measurable	Achievable	Realistic/Relevant	Time-bound

Use positive language to rewrite your finalized goal including the SMART elements from above.

_____

_____

What's your motivation?

_____

_____

Supports objectives: _____

Define this goal.

_____

_____

_____

_____

_____

_____

Success Checklist
Prework
Build SMART Goal
Know Why
Develop Details
Identify Resources
Develop Action Plan
Work
Visualize
Take Action
Achieve Goal!
Postwork
Celebrate
Evaluate

Identify resources and skills available and/or needed.

_____   _____

_____   _____

_____   _____

_____   _____

Action Plan	
Steps To Take	**Timeline**

Reward:

_____

Evaluation notes and lessons learned:

_____

_____

_____

_____

_____

_____

_____

_____

_____

_____

Goal # _____

_____

Specific	Measurable	Achievable	Realistic/Relevant	Time-bound

Use positive language to rewrite your finalized goal including the SMART elements from above.

_____

_____

What's your motivation?

_____

_____

Supports objectives: _____

Define this goal.

_____

_____

_____

_____

_____

Success Checklist
Prework
Build SMART Goal
Know Why
Develop Details
Identify Resources
Develop Action Plan
Work
Visualize
Take Action
Achieve Goal!
Postwork
Celebrate
Evaluate

Identify resources and skills available and/or needed.

_____   _____

_____   _____

_____   _____

_____   _____

Action Plan	
Steps To Take	**Timeline**

Reward:

_____

Evaluation notes and lessons learned:

_____

_____

_____

_____

_____

_____

_____

_____

_____

_____

Goal # _____

Specific	Measurable	Achievable	Realistic/Relevant	Time-bound

Use positive language to rewrite your finalized goal including the SMART elements from above.

_____
_____

What's your motivation?

_____
_____

Supports objectives: _____

Define this goal.

_____
_____
_____
_____
_____
_____

Success Checklist
Prework
Build SMART Goal
Know Why
Develop Details
Identify Resources
Develop Action Plan
Work
Visualize
Take Action
Achieve Goal!
Postwork
Celebrate
Evaluate

Identify resources and skills available and/or needed.

_____   _____
_____   _____
_____   _____
_____   _____

Action Plan	
Steps To Take	**Timeline**

Reward:

_____

Evaluation notes and lessons learned:

_____
_____
_____
_____
_____
_____
_____
_____
_____
_____
_____

☐ _____
Date Completed

Goal # _____

_____

Specific	Measurable	Achievable	Realistic/Relevant	Time-bound

Use positive language to rewrite your finalized goal including the SMART elements from above.

_____
_____

What's your motivation?

_____
_____

Supports objectives: _____

Define this goal.

_____
_____
_____
_____
_____
_____

Success Checklist
Prework
Build SMART Goal
Know Why
Develop Details
Identify Resources
Develop Action Plan
Work
Visualize
Take Action
Achieve Goal!
Postwork
Celebrate
Evaluate

Identify resources and skills available and/or needed.

_____   _____
_____   _____
_____   _____
_____   _____

Action Plan	
Steps To Take	**Timeline**

Reward:

_____

Evaluation notes and lessons learned:

_____
_____
_____
_____
_____
_____
_____
_____
_____
_____

Goal # _____

Specific	Measurable	Achievable	Realistic/Relevant	Time-bound

Use positive language to rewrite your finalized goal including the SMART elements from above.

_____

_____

What's your motivation?

_____

_____

Supports objectives: _____

Define this goal.

_____

_____

_____

_____

_____

_____

Success Checklist
Prework
Build SMART Goal
Know Why
Develop Details
Identify Resources
Develop Action Plan
Work
Visualize
Take Action
Achieve Goal!
Postwork
Celebrate
Evaluate

Identify resources and skills available and/or needed.

_____   _____

_____   _____

_____   _____

_____   _____

Action Plan	
Steps To Take	**Timeline**

Reward:

_____

Evaluation notes and lessons learned:

_____

_____

_____

_____

_____

_____

_____

_____

_____

☐ _____
Date Completed

Goal # _____

_____

Specific	Measurable	Achievable	Realistic/Relevant	Time-bound

Use positive language to rewrite your finalized goal including the SMART elements from above.

_____

_____

What's your motivation?

_____

_____

Supports objectives: _____

Define this goal.

_____

_____

_____

_____

_____

_____

Success Checklist
Prework
Build SMART Goal
Know Why
Develop Details
Identify Resources
Develop Action Plan
Work
Visualize
Take Action
Achieve Goal!
Postwork
Celebrate
Evaluate

Identify resources and skills available and/or needed.

_____   _____

_____   _____

_____   _____

_____   _____

Action Plan	
Steps To Take	**Timeline**

Reward:

_____

Evaluation notes and lessons learned:

_____

_____

_____

_____

_____

_____

_____

_____

_____

_____

_____

Goal # _____

_____

Specific	Measurable	Achievable	Realistic/Relevant	Time-bound

Use positive language to rewrite your finalized goal including the SMART elements from above.

_____

_____

What's your motivation?

_____

_____

Supports objectives: _____

Define this goal.

_____

_____

_____

_____

_____

_____

Success Checklist
Prework
Build SMART Goal
Know Why
Develop Details
Identify Resources
Develop Action Plan
Work
Visualize
Take Action
Achieve Goal!
Postwork
Celebrate
Evaluate

Identify resources and skills available and/or needed.

_____   _____

_____   _____

_____   _____

_____   _____

Action Plan	
Steps To Take	**Timeline**

Reward:

_____

Evaluation notes and lessons learned:

_____

_____

_____

_____

_____

_____

_____

_____

_____

_____

_____

☐ _____
Date Completed

Goal # _____

_____

Specific	Measurable	Achievable	Realistic/Relevant	Time-bound

Use positive language to rewrite your finalized goal including the SMART elements from above.

_____

_____

What's your motivation?

_____

_____

Supports objectives: _____

Define this goal.

_____

_____

_____

_____

_____

_____

Success Checklist
Prework
Build SMART Goal
Know Why
Develop Details
Identify Resources
Develop Action Plan
Work
Visualize
Take Action
Achieve Goal!
Postwork
Celebrate
Evaluate

Identify resources and skills available and/or needed.

_____   _____

_____   _____

_____   _____

_____   _____

Action Plan	
Steps To Take	**Timeline**

Reward:

_____

Evaluation notes and lessons learned:

_____

_____

_____

_____

_____

_____

_____

_____

_____

_____

_____

Goal # _____

☐ _____
Date Completed

Specific	Measurable	Achievable	Realistic/Relevant	Time-bound

Use positive language to rewrite your finalized goal including the SMART elements from above.

_____

_____

What's your motivation?

_____

_____

Supports objectives: _____

Define this goal.

_____

_____

_____

_____

_____

_____

Success Checklist
Prework
Build SMART Goal
Know Why
Develop Details
Identify Resources
Develop Action Plan
Work
Visualize
Take Action
Achieve Goal!
Postwork
Celebrate
Evaluate

Identify resources and skills available and/or needed.

_____   _____

_____   _____

_____   _____

_____   _____

Action Plan	
Steps To Take	**Timeline**

Reward:

_____

Evaluation notes and lessons learned:

_____

_____

_____

_____

_____

_____

_____

_____

_____

_____

☐ _____		Goal # _____		
Date Completed				

_____

Specific	Measurable	Achievable	Realistic/Relevant	Time-bound

Use positive language to rewrite your finalized goal including the SMART elements from above.

_____

_____

What's your motivation?

_____

_____

Supports objectives: _____

Define this goal.

_____

_____

_____

_____

_____

Success Checklist
Prework
Build SMART Goal
Know Why
Develop Details
Identify Resources
Develop Action Plan
Work
Visualize
Take Action
Achieve Goal!
Postwork
Celebrate
Evaluate

Identify resources and skills available and/or needed.

_____   _____

_____   _____

_____   _____

_____   _____

Action Plan	
Steps To Take	**Timeline**

Reward:

_____

Evaluation notes and lessons learned:

_____

_____

_____

_____

_____

_____

_____

_____

_____

_____

Goal # _____

_____

Specific	Measurable	Achievable	Realistic/Relevant	Time-bound

Use positive language to rewrite your finalized goal including the SMART elements from above.

_____
_____

What's your motivation?

_____
_____

Supports objectives: _____

Define this goal.

_____
_____
_____
_____
_____
_____

Success Checklist
Prework
Build SMART Goal
Know Why
Develop Details
Identify Resources
Develop Action Plan
Work
Visualize
Take Action
Achieve Goal!
Postwork
Celebrate
Evaluate

Identify resources and skills available and/or needed.

_____   _____
_____   _____
_____   _____
_____   _____

Action Plan	
Steps To Take	**Timeline**

Reward:

_____

Evaluation notes and lessons learned:

_____
_____
_____
_____
_____
_____
_____
_____
_____
_____
_____

☐ _____
Date Completed

Goal # _____

_____

Specific	Measurable	Achievable	Realistic/Relevant	Time-bound

Use positive language to rewrite your finalized goal including the SMART elements from above.

_____
_____

What's your motivation?

_____
_____

Supports objectives: _____

Define this goal.

_____
_____
_____
_____
_____
_____

Success Checklist
Prework
Build SMART Goal
Know Why
Develop Details
Identify Resources
Develop Action Plan
Work
Visualize
Take Action
Achieve Goal!
Postwork
Celebrate
Evaluate

Identify resources and skills available and/or needed.

_____   _____
_____   _____
_____   _____
_____   _____

Action Plan	
Steps To Take	**Timeline**

Reward:

_____

Evaluation notes and lessons learned:

_____
_____
_____
_____
_____
_____
_____
_____
_____
_____

Complex Goals

Goal # _____

☐ _____
Date Completed

Pre-Work

Specific	Measurable	Achievable	Realistic/Relevant	Time-bound

Use positive language to rewrite your finalized goal including the SMART elements from above.

_____

_____

What's your motivation? Why do you want to achieve this goal? (Also, do you want to achieve it for yourself or because someone else wants it for you?)

_____

_____

_____

_____

This goals supports objectives: _____

Define this goal. Describe, *in vivid detail*, exactly what you want and what your success looks and feels likes. Use as many senses in the description as possible. Make, model, size, shape, color, year, location, etc.. See, hear, and feel. Use details, details, details!

_____

_____

_____

_____

_____

_____

_____

_____

_____

_____

_____

_____

_____

_____

_____

Success Checklist
Prework
Build SMART Goal
Understand Why
Develop Details
Identify Strengths & Weaknesses
Identify Support
Identify Reward
Assess Commitment
Identify Resources
Identify Changes
Develop Action Plan & Timeline
Work
Visualize & Plant the Seed
Take the 1st Step
Build Affirmation Cards
Track Habits for 30 Days
Execute Plan
Phase 1
Phase 2
Phase 3
Phase 4
Achieve Goal!
Postwork
Celebrate
Evaluate

Have you gotten a clear mental image of this goal? If not what additional details will bring greater clarity?

_____

_____

_____

Can you see yourself achieving this goal? _____

How will you know when you've achieved this goal?

_____

_____

_____

_____

Have you attempted this goal before? _____

What barriers have you encountered in the past and/or what obstacles can you anticipate? How will you overcome them?

Barriers/Obstacles/Fears | How will you overcome them?

Barriers/Obstacles/Fears	How will you overcome them?
_____	_____
_____	_____
_____	_____
_____	_____
_____	_____

What assets and advantages do you have?

Assets/Advantages	How can you use these?
_____	_____
_____	_____
_____	_____
_____	_____
_____	_____

Are there any feelings of pain or pleasure around this goal?

Pain/Pleasure	How can you use these emotions in your motivation?
_____	_____
_____	_____
_____	_____
_____	_____
_____	_____

How will you benefit from achieving this goal?

_____

_____

_____

_____

How might this achievement improve how you feel about yourself?

_____

_____

_____

_____

How will you reward yourself when you've achieved this goal?

_____

_____

_____

_____

_____

Who has already achieved this goal that you may be able to model? _____

Are you willing to research their process and adapt it to your needs? _____

Where else might you find assistance? _____

Who will support you in this process? _____

Rate the following on a scale from 1 – 10 (1 = low and 10 = high) to determine your readiness to achieve this goal and discover areas to work on.

Are you ………………..

Committed	_____	Willing to sacrifice	_____	Willing to work now?	_____
Ready	_____	Disciplined	_____	Do you believe it?	_____
Deserving	_____	Consistent	_____	Focused	_____
Dedicated	_____	Capable	_____	Organized	_____
Supported	_____	Confident	_____	Positive	_____

Are you willing to schedule dedicated time to work on this goal daily? _____ If, so how much? _____

List five affirmations you will use to help you achieve this goal.

_____

_____

_____

_____

_____

Accept this goal as already true and write a thank you note to yourself for doing the work and to the universe/god for helping you achieve it.

_____

_____

_____

_____

Describe any positive feelings/emotions you feel around this goal now.

_____

_____

_____

Are you ready to take action towards this goal? _____

If not now, what will help you become ready?

_____

_____

_____

What does success look like?
Doodle, Notes, Images, Brainstorm, Mindmap

Visualize Success

Work

When will you begin working on this?_____

Have you added this goal to your vision board? _____ If not, when will you add it? _____

Where are you today compared to where you want to be with this goal? How can you get there?

Current Status	Goal	Difference/Actions Needed
_____	_____	_____
_____	_____	_____
_____	_____	_____
_____	_____	_____
_____	_____	_____

What skills and resources are already available to you and how can you use them?

Skills/Resources	How can you use it?
_____	_____
_____	_____
_____	_____
_____	_____

What skills and resources do you need and how might you acquire them?

Skills/Resources	How will you acquire it?
_____	_____
_____	_____
_____	_____
_____	_____
_____	_____

List any milestones along this journey.	How will you measure your successes and progress?
_____	_____
_____	
_____	How will you hold yourself accountable?
_____	_____
_____	_____

What action will you take today? _____

What daily actions are required (habits)? Identify keystone habits.

Stop	Start	Continue	Increase	Limit

Action Plan

	Steps to Take/Checklist	Timeline
PHASE 1		Start Date:
PHASE 2		
PHASE 3		
PHASE 4		

30-Day Habit Tracker
Goal

		Round 1																														
Habit	Start Date															Day																
1.		1	2	3	4	5	6	7	8	9	10	11	12	13	14	15	16	17	18	19	20	21	22	23	24	25	26	27	28	29	30
2.		1	2	3	4	5	6	7	8	9	10	11	12	13	14	15	16	17	18	19	20	21	22	23	24	25	26	27	28	29	30
3.		1	2	3	4	5	6	7	8	9	10	11	12	13	14	15	16	17	18	19	20	21	22	23	24	25	26	27	28	29	30
4.		1	2	3	4	5	6	7	8	9	10	11	12	13	14	15	16	17	18	19	20	21	22	23	24	25	26	27	28	29	30
5.		1	2	3	4	5	6	7	8	9	10	11	12	13	14	15	16	17	18	19	20	21	22	23	24	25	26	27	28	29	30

		Round 2																														
Habit	Start Date															Day																
1.		1	2	3	4	5	6	7	8	9	10	11	12	13	14	15	16	17	18	19	20	21	22	23	24	25	26	27	28	29	30
2.		1	2	3	4	5	6	7	8	9	10	11	12	13	14	15	16	17	18	19	20	21	22	23	24	25	26	27	28	29	30
3.		1	2	3	4	5	6	7	8	9	10	11	12	13	14	15	16	17	18	19	20	21	22	23	24	25	26	27	28	29	30
4.		1	2	3	4	5	6	7	8	9	10	11	12	13	14	15	16	17	18	19	20	21	22	23	24	25	26	27	28	29	30
5.		1	2	3	4	5	6	7	8	9	10	11	12	13	14	15	16	17	18	19	20	21	22	23	24	25	26	27	28	29	30

		Round 3																														
Habit	Start Date															Day																
1.		1	2	3	4	5	6	7	8	9	10	11	12	13	14	15	16	17	18	19	20	21	22	23	24	25	26	27	28	29	30
2.		1	2	3	4	5	6	7	8	9	10	11	12	13	14	15	16	17	18	19	20	21	22	23	24	25	26	27	28	29	30
3.		1	2	3	4	5	6	7	8	9	10	11	12	13	14	15	16	17	18	19	20	21	22	23	24	25	26	27	28	29	30
4.		1	2	3	4	5	6	7	8	9	10	11	12	13	14	15	16	17	18	19	20	21	22	23	24	25	26	27	28	29	30
5.		1	2	3	4	5	6	7	8	9	10	11	12	13	14	15	16	17	18	19	20	21	22	23	24	25	26	27	28	29	30

		Round 4																														
Habit	Start Date															Day																
1.		1	2	3	4	5	6	7	8	9	10	11	12	13	14	15	16	17	18	19	20	21	22	23	24	25	26	27	28	29	30
2.		1	2	3	4	5	6	7	8	9	10	11	12	13	14	15	16	17	18	19	20	21	22	23	24	25	26	27	28	29	30
3.		1	2	3	4	5	6	7	8	9	10	11	12	13	14	15	16	17	18	19	20	21	22	23	24	25	26	27	28	29	30
4.		1	2	3	4	5	6	7	8	9	10	11	12	13	14	15	16	17	18	19	20	21	22	23	24	25	26	27	28	29	30
5.		1	2	3	4	5	6	7	8	9	10	11	12	13	14	15	16	17	18	19	20	21	22	23	24	25	26	27	28	29	30

		Round 5																														
Habit	Start Date															Day																
1.		1	2	3	4	5	6	7	8	9	10	11	12	13	14	15	16	17	18	19	20	21	22	23	24	25	26	27	28	29	30
2.		1	2	3	4	5	6	7	8	9	10	11	12	13	14	15	16	17	18	19	20	21	22	23	24	25	26	27	28	29	30
3.		1	2	3	4	5	6	7	8	9	10	11	12	13	14	15	16	17	18	19	20	21	22	23	24	25	26	27	28	29	30
4.		1	2	3	4	5	6	7	8	9	10	11	12	13	14	15	16	17	18	19	20	21	22	23	24	25	26	27	28	29	30
5.		1	2	3	4	5	6	7	8	9	10	11	12	13	14	15	16	17	18	19	20	21	22	23	24	25	26	27	28	29	30

		Round 6																														
Habit	Start Date															Day																
1.		1	2	3	4	5	6	7	8	9	10	11	12	13	14	15	16	17	18	19	20	21	22	23	24	25	26	27	28	29	30
2.		1	2	3	4	5	6	7	8	9	10	11	12	13	14	15	16	17	18	19	20	21	22	23	24	25	26	27	28	29	30
3.		1	2	3	4	5	6	7	8	9	10	11	12	13	14	15	16	17	18	19	20	21	22	23	24	25	26	27	28	29	30
4.		1	2	3	4	5	6	7	8	9	10	11	12	13	14	15	16	17	18	19	20	21	22	23	24	25	26	27	28	29	30
5.		1	2	3	4	5	6	7	8	9	10	11	12	13	14	15	16	17	18	19	20	21	22	23	24	25	26	27	28	29	30

Post-Work

Congratulations! You've achieved your goal. Now, celebrate your success. You deserve it!

After the celebration, it's time for evaluation. Take a look back on what you've experienced around this goal. Note any observations, obstacles, and lessons learned and how you apply them in the future.

Was the experience what you expected it to be? If not, why?_____

_____
_____
_____

What happened with this goal and its execution? Did anything stand out?

_____
_____
_____
_____
_____
_____

Did everything go as planned? _____   Did you stick to the timeline? _____
What went well?

_____
_____
_____
_____

What could've gone better?   How can you make adjustments in the future?

_____   _____
_____   _____
_____   _____
_____   _____

What lessons did you learn?   How will you apply them?

_____   _____
_____   _____
_____   _____
_____   _____

How have you grown from this experience?

_____
_____
_____
_____

How will you maintain this success?

_____
_____
_____
_____

Goal # _____

Pre-Work

Specific	Measurable	Achievable	Realistic/Relevant	Time-bound

Use positive language to rewrite your finalized goal including the SMART elements from above.

_____

_____

What's your motivation? Why do you want to achieve this goal? (Also, do you want to achieve it for yourself or because someone else wants it for you?)

_____

_____

_____

_____

This goals supports objectives: _____

Define this goal. Describe, *in vivid detail*, exactly what you want and what your success looks and feels likes. Use as many senses in the description as possible. Make, model, size, shape, color, year, location, etc.. See, hear, and feel. Use details, details, details!

_____

_____

_____

_____

_____

_____

_____

_____

_____

_____

_____

_____

_____

_____

_____

_____

Success Checklist
Prework
Build SMART Goal
Understand Why
Develop Details
Identify Strengths & Weaknesses
Identify Support
Identify Reward
Assess Commitment
Identify Resources
Identify Changes
Develop Action Plan & Timeline
Work
Visualize & Plant the Seed
Take the 1st Step
Build Affirmation Cards
Track Habits for 30 Days
Execute Plan
Phase 1
Phase 2
Phase 3
Phase 4
Achieve Goal!
Postwork
Celebrate
Evaluate

Have you gotten a clear mental image of this goal? If not what additional details will bring greater clarity?

_____
_____
_____

Can you see yourself achieving this goal? _____

How will you know when you've achieved this goal?

_____
_____
_____
_____

Have you attempted this goal before? _____

What barriers have you encountered in the past and/or what obstacles can you anticipate? How will you overcome them?

Barriers/Obstacles/Fears	How will you overcome them?
_____	_____
_____	_____
_____	_____
_____	_____
_____	_____

What assets and advantages do you have?

Assets/Advantages	How can you use these?
_____	_____
_____	_____
_____	_____
_____	_____
_____	_____

Are there any feelings of pain or pleasure around this goal?

Pain/Pleasure	How can you use these emotions in your motivation?
_____	_____
_____	_____
_____	_____
_____	_____
_____	_____

How will you benefit from achieving this goal?

_____
_____
_____
_____

How might this achievement improve how you feel about yourself?

_____
_____
_____
_____

How will you reward yourself when you've achieved this goal?

_____

_____

_____

_____

_____

Who has already achieved this goal that you may be able to model? _____

Are you willing to research their process and adapt it to your needs? _____

Where else might you find assistance? _____

Who will support you in this process? _____

Rate the following on a scale from 1 – 10 (1 = low and 10 = high) to determine your readiness to achieve this goal and discover areas to work on.

Are you ………………

Committed	_____	Willing to sacrifice	_____	Willing to work now?	_____
Ready	_____	Disciplined	_____	Do you believe it?	_____
Deserving	_____	Consistent	_____	Focused	_____
Dedicated	_____	Capable	_____	Organized	_____
Supported	_____	Confident	_____	Positive	_____

Are you willing to schedule dedicated time to work on this goal daily? _____ If, so how much? _____

List five affirmations you will use to help you achieve this goal.

_____

_____

_____

_____

_____

Accept this goal as already true and write a thank you note to yourself for doing the work and to the universe/god for helping you achieve it.

_____

_____

_____

_____

_____

Describe any positive feelings/emotions you feel around this goal now.

_____

_____

_____

_____

Are you ready to take action towards this goal? _____

If not now, what will help you become ready?

_____

_____

_____

What does success look like?
Doodle, Notes, Images, Brainstorm, Mindmap

Visualize Success

Work

When will you begin working on this?_____

Have you added this goal to your vision board? _____ If not, when will you add it? _____

Where are you today compared to where you want to be with this goal? How can you get there?

Current Status	Goal	Difference/Actions Needed
_____	_____	_____
_____	_____	_____
_____	_____	_____
_____	_____	_____
_____	_____	_____

What skills and resources are already available to you and how can you use them?

Skills/Resources	How can you use it?
_____	_____
_____	_____
_____	_____
_____	_____

What skills and resources do you need and how might you acquire them?

Skills/Resources	How will you acquire it?
_____	_____
_____	_____
_____	_____
_____	_____

List any milestones along this journey.

How will you measure your successes and progress?

_____

_____

How will you hold yourself accountable?

_____

_____

What action will you take today? _____

What daily actions are required (habits)? Identify keystone habits.

Stop	Start	Continue	Increase	Limit

Action Plan

	Steps to Take/Checklist	Timeline
PHASE 1		Start Date:
PHASE 2		
PHASE 3		
PHASE 4		

30-Day Habit Tracker
Goal

Round 1			

Habit	Start Date	Day
1.		1 2 3 4 5 6 7 8 9 10 11 12 13 14 15 16 17 18 19 20 21 22 23 24 25 26 27 28 29 30
2.		1 2 3 4 5 6 7 8 9 10 11 12 13 14 15 16 17 18 19 20 21 22 23 24 25 26 27 28 29 30
3.		1 2 3 4 5 6 7 8 9 10 11 12 13 14 15 16 17 18 19 20 21 22 23 24 25 26 27 28 29 30
4.		1 2 3 4 5 6 7 8 9 10 11 12 13 14 15 16 17 18 19 20 21 22 23 24 25 26 27 28 29 30
5.		1 2 3 4 5 6 7 8 9 10 11 12 13 14 15 16 17 18 19 20 21 22 23 24 25 26 27 28 29 30

Round 2			

Habit	Start Date	Day
1.		1 2 3 4 5 6 7 8 9 10 11 12 13 14 15 16 17 18 19 20 21 22 23 24 25 26 27 28 29 30
2.		1 2 3 4 5 6 7 8 9 10 11 12 13 14 15 16 17 18 19 20 21 22 23 24 25 26 27 28 29 30
3.		1 2 3 4 5 6 7 8 9 10 11 12 13 14 15 16 17 18 19 20 21 22 23 24 25 26 27 28 29 30
4.		1 2 3 4 5 6 7 8 9 10 11 12 13 14 15 16 17 18 19 20 21 22 23 24 25 26 27 28 29 30
5.		1 2 3 4 5 6 7 8 9 10 11 12 13 14 15 16 17 18 19 20 21 22 23 24 25 26 27 28 29 30

Round 3			

Habit	Start Date	Day
1.		1 2 3 4 5 6 7 8 9 10 11 12 13 14 15 16 17 18 19 20 21 22 23 24 25 26 27 28 29 30
2.		1 2 3 4 5 6 7 8 9 10 11 12 13 14 15 16 17 18 19 20 21 22 23 24 25 26 27 28 29 30
3.		1 2 3 4 5 6 7 8 9 10 11 12 13 14 15 16 17 18 19 20 21 22 23 24 25 26 27 28 29 30
4.		1 2 3 4 5 6 7 8 9 10 11 12 13 14 15 16 17 18 19 20 21 22 23 24 25 26 27 28 29 30
5.		1 2 3 4 5 6 7 8 9 10 11 12 13 14 15 16 17 18 19 20 21 22 23 24 25 26 27 28 29 30

Round 4			

Habit	Start Date	Day
1.		1 2 3 4 5 6 7 8 9 10 11 12 13 14 15 16 17 18 19 20 21 22 23 24 25 26 27 28 29 30
2.		1 2 3 4 5 6 7 8 9 10 11 12 13 14 15 16 17 18 19 20 21 22 23 24 25 26 27 28 29 30
3.		1 2 3 4 5 6 7 8 9 10 11 12 13 14 15 16 17 18 19 20 21 22 23 24 25 26 27 28 29 30
4.		1 2 3 4 5 6 7 8 9 10 11 12 13 14 15 16 17 18 19 20 21 22 23 24 25 26 27 28 29 30
5.		1 2 3 4 5 6 7 8 9 10 11 12 13 14 15 16 17 18 19 20 21 22 23 24 25 26 27 28 29 30

Round 5			

Habit	Start Date	Day
1.		1 2 3 4 5 6 7 8 9 10 11 12 13 14 15 16 17 18 19 20 21 22 23 24 25 26 27 28 29 30
2.		1 2 3 4 5 6 7 8 9 10 11 12 13 14 15 16 17 18 19 20 21 22 23 24 25 26 27 28 29 30
3.		1 2 3 4 5 6 7 8 9 10 11 12 13 14 15 16 17 18 19 20 21 22 23 24 25 26 27 28 29 30
4.		1 2 3 4 5 6 7 8 9 10 11 12 13 14 15 16 17 18 19 20 21 22 23 24 25 26 27 28 29 30
5.		1 2 3 4 5 6 7 8 9 10 11 12 13 14 15 16 17 18 19 20 21 22 23 24 25 26 27 28 29 30

Round 6			

Habit	Start Date	Day
1.		1 2 3 4 5 6 7 8 9 10 11 12 13 14 15 16 17 18 19 20 21 22 23 24 25 26 27 28 29 30
2.		1 2 3 4 5 6 7 8 9 10 11 12 13 14 15 16 17 18 19 20 21 22 23 24 25 26 27 28 29 30
3.		1 2 3 4 5 6 7 8 9 10 11 12 13 14 15 16 17 18 19 20 21 22 23 24 25 26 27 28 29 30
4.		1 2 3 4 5 6 7 8 9 10 11 12 13 14 15 16 17 18 19 20 21 22 23 24 25 26 27 28 29 30
5.		1 2 3 4 5 6 7 8 9 10 11 12 13 14 15 16 17 18 19 20 21 22 23 24 25 26 27 28 29 30

Post-Work

Congratulations! You've achieved your goal. Now, celebrate your success. You deserve it!

After the celebration, it's time for evaluation. Take a look back on what you've experienced around this goal. Note any observations, obstacles, and lessons learned and how you apply them in the future.

Was the experience what you expected it to be? If not, why?_____

_____
_____
_____

What happened with this goal and its execution? Did anything stand out?

_____
_____
_____
_____
_____
_____

Did everything go as planned? _____   Did you stick to the timeline? _____
What went well?

_____
_____
_____
_____

What could've gone better?   How can you make adjustments in the future?

_____   _____
_____   _____
_____   _____
_____   _____

What lessons did you learn?   How will you apply them?

_____   _____
_____   _____
_____   _____
_____   _____

How have you grown from this experience?

_____
_____
_____

How will you maintain this success?

_____
_____
_____
_____

Goal # _____

Pre-Work

Specific	Measurable	Achievable	Realistic/Relevant	Time-bound

Use positive language to rewrite your finalized goal including the SMART elements from above.

_____

_____

What's your motivation? Why do you want to achieve this goal? (Also, do you want to achieve it for yourself or because someone else wants it for you?)

_____

_____

_____

_____

_____

This goals supports objectives: _____

Define this goal. Describe, *in vivid detail*, <u>exactly</u> what you want and what your success looks and feels likes. Use as many senses in the description as possible. Make, model, size, shape, color, year, location, etc.. See, hear, and feel. Use details, details, details!

Success Checklist
Prework
Build SMART Goal
Understand Why
Develop Details
Identify Strengths & Weaknesses
Identify Support
Identify Reward
Assess Commitment
Identify Resources
Identify Changes
Develop Action Plan & Timeline
Work
Visualize & Plant the Seed
Take the 1st Step
Build Affirmation Cards
Track Habits for 30 Days
Execute Plan
Phase 1
Phase 2
Phase 3
Phase 4
Achieve Goal!
Postwork
Celebrate
Evaluate

Have you gotten a clear mental image of this goal? If not what additional details will bring greater clarity?

_____
_____
_____

Can you see yourself achieving this goal? _____

How will you know when you've achieved this goal?

_____
_____
_____
_____

Have you attempted this goal before? _____

What barriers have you encountered in the past and/or what obstacles can you anticipate? How will you overcome them?

Barriers/Obstacles/Fears	How will you overcome them?
_____	_____
_____	_____
_____	_____
_____	_____
_____	_____

What assets and advantages do you have?

Assets/Advantages	How can you use these?
_____	_____
_____	_____
_____	_____
_____	_____
_____	_____

Are there any feelings of pain or pleasure around this goal?

Pain/Pleasure	How can you use these emotions in your motivation?
_____	_____
_____	_____
_____	_____
_____	_____
_____	_____

How will you benefit from achieving this goal?

_____
_____
_____
_____

How might this achievement improve how you feel about yourself?

_____
_____
_____
_____

How will you reward yourself when you've achieved this goal?

_____
_____
_____
_____
_____

Who has already achieved this goal that you may be able to model? _____

Are you willing to research their process and adapt it to your needs? _____

Where else might you find assistance? _____

Who will support you in this process? _____

Rate the following on a scale from 1 – 10 (1 = low and 10 = high) to determine your readiness to achieve this goal and discover areas to work on.

Are you ....

Committed	_____	Willing to sacrifice	_____	Willing to work now?	_____
Ready	_____	Disciplined	_____	Do you believe it?	_____
Deserving	_____	Consistent	_____	Focused	_____
Dedicated	_____	Capable	_____	Organized	_____
Supported	_____	Confident	_____	Positive	_____

Are you willing to schedule dedicated time to work on this goal daily? _____ If, so how much? _____

List five affirmations you will use to help you achieve this goal.

_____
_____
_____
_____
_____

Accept this goal as already true and write a thank you note to yourself for doing the work and to the universe/god for helping you achieve it.

_____
_____
_____
_____
_____

Describe any positive feelings/emotions you feel around this goal now.

_____
_____
_____
_____

Are you ready to take action towards this goal? _____

If not now, what will help you become ready?

_____
_____
_____

What does success look like?
Doodle, Notes, Images, Brainstorm, Mindmap

Visualize Success

Work

When will you begin working on this?_____

Have you added this goal to your vision board? _____ If not, when will you add it? _____

Where are you today compared to where you want to be with this goal? How can you get there?

Current Status	Goal	Difference/Actions Needed
_____	_____	_____
_____	_____	_____
_____	_____	_____
_____	_____	_____
_____	_____	_____

What skills and resources are already available to you and how can you use them?

Skills/Resources	How can you use it?
_____	_____
_____	_____
_____	_____
_____	_____

What skills and resources do you need and how might you acquire them?

Skills/Resources	How will you acquire it?
_____	_____
_____	_____
_____	_____
_____	_____

List any milestones along this journey.

_____

_____

How will you measure your successes and progress?

_____

_____

How will you hold yourself accountable?

_____

_____

What action will you take today? _____

What daily actions are required (habits)? Identify keystone habits.

Stop	Start	Continue	Increase	Limit

Action Plan

	Steps to Take/Checklist	Timeline
PHASE 1		Start Date:
PHASE 2		
PHASE 3		
PHASE 4		

30-Day Habit Tracker
Goal

Round 1																																		
Habit	**Start Date**	\multicolumn{33}{Day}

Habit	Start Date	Day
1.		1 2 3 4 5 6 7 8 9 10 11 12 13 14 15 16 17 18 19 20 21 22 23 24 25 26 27 28 29 30
2.		1 2 3 4 5 6 7 8 9 10 11 12 13 14 15 16 17 18 19 20 21 22 23 24 25 26 27 28 29 30
3.		1 2 3 4 5 6 7 8 9 10 11 12 13 14 15 16 17 18 19 20 21 22 23 24 25 26 27 28 29 30
4.		1 2 3 4 5 6 7 8 9 10 11 12 13 14 15 16 17 18 19 20 21 22 23 24 25 26 27 28 29 30
5.		1 2 3 4 5 6 7 8 9 10 11 12 13 14 15 16 17 18 19 20 21 22 23 24 25 26 27 28 29 30

Round 2

Habit	Start Date	Day
1.		1 2 3 4 5 6 7 8 9 10 11 12 13 14 15 16 17 18 19 20 21 22 23 24 25 26 27 28 29 30
2.		1 2 3 4 5 6 7 8 9 10 11 12 13 14 15 16 17 18 19 20 21 22 23 24 25 26 27 28 29 30
3.		1 2 3 4 5 6 7 8 9 10 11 12 13 14 15 16 17 18 19 20 21 22 23 24 25 26 27 28 29 30
4.		1 2 3 4 5 6 7 8 9 10 11 12 13 14 15 16 17 18 19 20 21 22 23 24 25 26 27 28 29 30
5.		1 2 3 4 5 6 7 8 9 10 11 12 13 14 15 16 17 18 19 20 21 22 23 24 25 26 27 28 29 30

Round 3

Habit	Start Date	Day
1.		1 2 3 4 5 6 7 8 9 10 11 12 13 14 15 16 17 18 19 20 21 22 23 24 25 26 27 28 29 30
2.		1 2 3 4 5 6 7 8 9 10 11 12 13 14 15 16 17 18 19 20 21 22 23 24 25 26 27 28 29 30
3.		1 2 3 4 5 6 7 8 9 10 11 12 13 14 15 16 17 18 19 20 21 22 23 24 25 26 27 28 29 30
4.		1 2 3 4 5 6 7 8 9 10 11 12 13 14 15 16 17 18 19 20 21 22 23 24 25 26 27 28 29 30
5.		1 2 3 4 5 6 7 8 9 10 11 12 13 14 15 16 17 18 19 20 21 22 23 24 25 26 27 28 29 30

Round 4

Habit	Start Date	Day
1.		1 2 3 4 5 6 7 8 9 10 11 12 13 14 15 16 17 18 19 20 21 22 23 24 25 26 27 28 29 30
2.		1 2 3 4 5 6 7 8 9 10 11 12 13 14 15 16 17 18 19 20 21 22 23 24 25 26 27 28 29 30
3.		1 2 3 4 5 6 7 8 9 10 11 12 13 14 15 16 17 18 19 20 21 22 23 24 25 26 27 28 29 30
4.		1 2 3 4 5 6 7 8 9 10 11 12 13 14 15 16 17 18 19 20 21 22 23 24 25 26 27 28 29 30
5.		1 2 3 4 5 6 7 8 9 10 11 12 13 14 15 16 17 18 19 20 21 22 23 24 25 26 27 28 29 30

Round 5

Habit	Start Date	Day
1.		1 2 3 4 5 6 7 8 9 10 11 12 13 14 15 16 17 18 19 20 21 22 23 24 25 26 27 28 29 30
2.		1 2 3 4 5 6 7 8 9 10 11 12 13 14 15 16 17 18 19 20 21 22 23 24 25 26 27 28 29 30
3.		1 2 3 4 5 6 7 8 9 10 11 12 13 14 15 16 17 18 19 20 21 22 23 24 25 26 27 28 29 30
4.		1 2 3 4 5 6 7 8 9 10 11 12 13 14 15 16 17 18 19 20 21 22 23 24 25 26 27 28 29 30
5.		1 2 3 4 5 6 7 8 9 10 11 12 13 14 15 16 17 18 19 20 21 22 23 24 25 26 27 28 29 30

Round 6

Habit	Start Date	Day
1.		1 2 3 4 5 6 7 8 9 10 11 12 13 14 15 16 17 18 19 20 21 22 23 24 25 26 27 28 29 30
2.		1 2 3 4 5 6 7 8 9 10 11 12 13 14 15 16 17 18 19 20 21 22 23 24 25 26 27 28 29 30
3.		1 2 3 4 5 6 7 8 9 10 11 12 13 14 15 16 17 18 19 20 21 22 23 24 25 26 27 28 29 30
4.		1 2 3 4 5 6 7 8 9 10 11 12 13 14 15 16 17 18 19 20 21 22 23 24 25 26 27 28 29 30
5.		1 2 3 4 5 6 7 8 9 10 11 12 13 14 15 16 17 18 19 20 21 22 23 24 25 26 27 28 29 30

Post-Work

Congratulations! You've achieved your goal. Now, celebrate your success. You deserve it!

After the celebration, it's time for evaluation. Take a look back on what you've experienced around this goal. Note any observations, obstacles, and lessons learned and how you apply them in the future.

Was the experience what you expected it to be? If not, why?_____

_____
_____
_____

 What happened with this goal and its execution? Did anything stand out?

_____
_____
_____
_____
_____
_____

Did everything go as planned? _____   Did you stick to the timeline? _____
What went well?

_____
_____
_____
_____

What could've gone better?   How can you make adjustments in the future?

_____   _____
_____   _____
_____   _____
_____   _____

What lessons did you learn?   How will you apply them?

_____   _____
_____   _____
_____   _____
_____   _____

How have you grown from this experience?

_____
_____
_____
_____

How will you maintain this success?

_____
_____
_____
_____

Goal # _____

Pre-Work

Specific	Measurable	Achievable	Realistic/Relevant	Time-bound

Use positive language to rewrite your finalized goal including the SMART elements from above.

_____

_____

What's your motivation? Why do you want to achieve this goal? (Also, do you want to achieve it for yourself or because someone else wants it for you?)

_____

_____

_____

_____

This goals supports objectives: _____

Define this goal. Describe, *in vivid detail*, <u>exactly</u> what you want and what your success looks and feels likes. Use as many senses in the description as possible. Make, model, size, shape, color, year, location, etc.. See, hear, and feel. Use details, details, details!

_____

_____

_____

_____

_____

_____

_____

_____

_____

_____

_____

_____

_____

_____

Success Checklist
Prework
Build SMART Goal
Understand Why
Develop Details
Identify Strengths & Weaknesses
Identify Support
Identify Reward
Assess Commitment
Identify Resources
Identify Changes
Develop Action Plan & Timeline
Work
Visualize & Plant the Seed
Take the 1st Step
Build Affirmation Cards
Track Habits for 30 Days
Execute Plan
Phase 1
Phase 2
Phase 3
Phase 4
Achieve Goal!
Postwork
Celebrate
Evaluate

Have you gotten a clear mental image of this goal? If not what additional details will bring greater clarity?

_____

_____

_____

Can you see yourself achieving this goal? _____

How will you know when you've achieved this goal?

_____

_____

_____

_____

Have you attempted this goal before? _____

What barriers have you encountered in the past and/or what obstacles can you anticipate? How will you overcome them?

Barriers/Obstacles/Fears	How will you overcome them?
_____	_____
_____	_____
_____	_____
_____	_____
_____	_____

What assets and advantages do you have?

Assets/Advantages	How can you use these?
_____	_____
_____	_____
_____	_____
_____	_____
_____	_____

Are there any feelings of pain or pleasure around this goal?

Pain/Pleasure	How can you use these emotions in your motivation?
_____	_____
_____	_____
_____	_____
_____	_____
_____	_____

How will you benefit from achieving this goal?

_____

_____

_____

_____

_____

How might this achievement improve how you feel about yourself?

_____

_____

_____

_____

How will you reward yourself when you've achieved this goal?

_____

_____

_____

_____

_____

Who has already achieved this goal that you may be able to model? _____

Are you willing to research their process and adapt it to your needs? _____

Where else might you find assistance? _____

Who will support you in this process? _____

Rate the following on a scale from 1 – 10 (1 = low and 10 = high) to determine your readiness to achieve this goal and discover areas to work on.

Are you ………………

Committed	_____	Willing to sacrifice	_____	Willing to work now?	_____
Ready	_____	Disciplined	_____	Do you believe it?	_____
Deserving	_____	Consistent	_____	Focused	_____
Dedicated	_____	Capable	_____	Organized	_____
Supported	_____	Confident	_____	Positive	_____

Are you willing to schedule dedicated time to work on this goal daily? _____ If, so how much? _____

List five affirmations you will use to help you achieve this goal.

_____

_____

_____

_____

_____

Accept this goal as already true and write a thank you note to yourself for doing the work and to the universe/god for helping you achieve it.

_____

_____

_____

_____

_____

Describe any positive feelings/emotions you feel around this goal now.

_____

_____

_____

_____

Are you ready to take action towards this goal? _____

If not now, what will help you become ready?

_____

_____

_____

What does success look like?
Doodle, Notes, Images, Brainstorm, Mindmap

Visualize Success

Work

When will you begin working on this?_____

Have you added this goal to your vision board? _____ If not, when will you add it? _____

Where are you today compared to where you want to be with this goal? How can you get there?

Current Status	Goal	Difference/Actions Needed
_____	_____	_____
_____	_____	_____
_____	_____	_____
_____	_____	_____
_____	_____	_____

What skills and resources are already available to you and how can you use them?

Skills/Resources   How can you use it?

_____   _____
_____   _____
_____   _____
_____   _____

What skills and resources do you need and how might you acquire them?

Skills/Resources   How will you acquire it?

_____   _____
_____   _____
_____   _____
_____   _____

List any milestones along this journey.   How will you measure your successes and progress?

_____   _____
_____   _____
_____   How will you hold yourself accountable?
_____
_____   _____
                                          _____

What action will you take today? _____

What daily actions are required (habits)? Identify keystone habits.

Stop	Start	Continue	Increase	Limit

Action Plan

	Steps to Take/Checklist	Timeline
PHASE 1		Start Date:
PHASE 2		
PHASE 3		
PHASE 4		

30-Day Habit Tracker
Goal

Round 1

Habit	Start Date	Day
1.		1 2 3 4 5 6 7 8 9 10 11 12 13 14 15 16 17 18 19 20 21 22 23 24 25 26 27 28 29 30
2.		1 2 3 4 5 6 7 8 9 10 11 12 13 14 15 16 17 18 19 20 21 22 23 24 25 26 27 28 29 30
3.		1 2 3 4 5 6 7 8 9 10 11 12 13 14 15 16 17 18 19 20 21 22 23 24 25 26 27 28 29 30
4.		1 2 3 4 5 6 7 8 9 10 11 12 13 14 15 16 17 18 19 20 21 22 23 24 25 26 27 28 29 30
5.		1 2 3 4 5 6 7 8 9 10 11 12 13 14 15 16 17 18 19 20 21 22 23 24 25 26 27 28 29 30

Round 2

Habit	Start Date	Day
1.		1 2 3 4 5 6 7 8 9 10 11 12 13 14 15 16 17 18 19 20 21 22 23 24 25 26 27 28 29 30
2.		1 2 3 4 5 6 7 8 9 10 11 12 13 14 15 16 17 18 19 20 21 22 23 24 25 26 27 28 29 30
3.		1 2 3 4 5 6 7 8 9 10 11 12 13 14 15 16 17 18 19 20 21 22 23 24 25 26 27 28 29 30
4.		1 2 3 4 5 6 7 8 9 10 11 12 13 14 15 16 17 18 19 20 21 22 23 24 25 26 27 28 29 30
5.		1 2 3 4 5 6 7 8 9 10 11 12 13 14 15 16 17 18 19 20 21 22 23 24 25 26 27 28 29 30

Round 3

Habit	Start Date	Day
1.		1 2 3 4 5 6 7 8 9 10 11 12 13 14 15 16 17 18 19 20 21 22 23 24 25 26 27 28 29 30
2.		1 2 3 4 5 6 7 8 9 10 11 12 13 14 15 16 17 18 19 20 21 22 23 24 25 26 27 28 29 30
3.		1 2 3 4 5 6 7 8 9 10 11 12 13 14 15 16 17 18 19 20 21 22 23 24 25 26 27 28 29 30
4.		1 2 3 4 5 6 7 8 9 10 11 12 13 14 15 16 17 18 19 20 21 22 23 24 25 26 27 28 29 30
5.		1 2 3 4 5 6 7 8 9 10 11 12 13 14 15 16 17 18 19 20 21 22 23 24 25 26 27 28 29 30

Round 4

Habit	Start Date	Day
1.		1 2 3 4 5 6 7 8 9 10 11 12 13 14 15 16 17 18 19 20 21 22 23 24 25 26 27 28 29 30
2.		1 2 3 4 5 6 7 8 9 10 11 12 13 14 15 16 17 18 19 20 21 22 23 24 25 26 27 28 29 30
3.		1 2 3 4 5 6 7 8 9 10 11 12 13 14 15 16 17 18 19 20 21 22 23 24 25 26 27 28 29 30
4.		1 2 3 4 5 6 7 8 9 10 11 12 13 14 15 16 17 18 19 20 21 22 23 24 25 26 27 28 29 30
5.		1 2 3 4 5 6 7 8 9 10 11 12 13 14 15 16 17 18 19 20 21 22 23 24 25 26 27 28 29 30

Round 5

Habit	Start Date	Day
1.		1 2 3 4 5 6 7 8 9 10 11 12 13 14 15 16 17 18 19 20 21 22 23 24 25 26 27 28 29 30
2.		1 2 3 4 5 6 7 8 9 10 11 12 13 14 15 16 17 18 19 20 21 22 23 24 25 26 27 28 29 30
3.		1 2 3 4 5 6 7 8 9 10 11 12 13 14 15 16 17 18 19 20 21 22 23 24 25 26 27 28 29 30
4.		1 2 3 4 5 6 7 8 9 10 11 12 13 14 15 16 17 18 19 20 21 22 23 24 25 26 27 28 29 30
5.		1 2 3 4 5 6 7 8 9 10 11 12 13 14 15 16 17 18 19 20 21 22 23 24 25 26 27 28 29 30

Round 6

Habit	Start Date	Day
1.		1 2 3 4 5 6 7 8 9 10 11 12 13 14 15 16 17 18 19 20 21 22 23 24 25 26 27 28 29 30
2.		1 2 3 4 5 6 7 8 9 10 11 12 13 14 15 16 17 18 19 20 21 22 23 24 25 26 27 28 29 30
3.		1 2 3 4 5 6 7 8 9 10 11 12 13 14 15 16 17 18 19 20 21 22 23 24 25 26 27 28 29 30
4.		1 2 3 4 5 6 7 8 9 10 11 12 13 14 15 16 17 18 19 20 21 22 23 24 25 26 27 28 29 30
5.		1 2 3 4 5 6 7 8 9 10 11 12 13 14 15 16 17 18 19 20 21 22 23 24 25 26 27 28 29 30

Post-Work

Congratulations! You've achieved your goal. Now, celebrate your success. You deserve it!

After the celebration, it's time for evaluation. Take a look back on what you've experienced around this goal. Note any observations, obstacles, and lessons learned and how you apply them in the future.

Was the experience what you expected it to be? If not, why?_____

_____
_____
_____

What happened with this goal and its execution? Did anything stand out?

_____
_____
_____
_____
_____
_____

Did everything go as planned? _____   Did you stick to the timeline? _____
What went well?

_____
_____
_____
_____

What could've gone better?   How can you make adjustments in the future?

_____   _____
_____   _____
_____   _____
_____   _____

What lessons did you learn?   How will you apply them?

_____   _____
_____   _____
_____   _____
_____   _____

How have you grown from this experience?

_____
_____
_____
_____

How will you maintain this success?

_____
_____
_____
_____

Goal # _____

Pre-Work

Specific	Measurable	Achievable	Realistic/Relevant	Time-bound

Use positive language to rewrite your finalized goal including the SMART elements from above.

_____

_____

What's your motivation? Why do you want to achieve this goal? (Also, do you want to achieve it for yourself or because someone else wants it for you?)

_____

_____

_____

_____

This goals supports objectives: _____

Define this goal. Describe, *in vivid detail*, <u>exactly</u> what you want and what your success looks and feels likes. Use as many senses in the description as possible. Make, model, size, shape, color, year, location, etc.. See, hear, and feel. Use details, details, details!

_____

_____

_____

_____

_____

_____

_____

_____

_____

_____

_____

_____

_____

_____

_____

Success Checklist
Prework
Build SMART Goal
Understand Why
Develop Details
Identify Strengths & Weaknesses
Identify Support
Identify Reward
Assess Commitment
Identify Resources
Identify Changes
Develop Action Plan & Timeline
Work
Visualize & Plant the Seed
Take the 1st Step
Build Affirmation Cards
Track Habits for 30 Days
Execute Plan
Phase 1
Phase 2
Phase 3
Phase 4
Achieve Goal!
Postwork
Celebrate
Evaluate

Have you gotten a clear mental image of this goal? If not what additional details will bring greater clarity?

_____
_____
_____

Can you see yourself achieving this goal? _____

How will you know when you've achieved this goal?

_____
_____
_____
_____

Have you attempted this goal before? _____

What barriers have you encountered in the past and/or what obstacles can you anticipate? How will you overcome them?

Barriers/Obstacles/Fears   How will you overcome them?

_____   _____
_____   _____
_____   _____
_____   _____
_____   _____

What assets and advantages do you have?

Assets/Advantages   How can you use these?

_____   _____
_____   _____
_____   _____
_____   _____
_____   _____

Are there any feelings of pain or pleasure around this goal?

Pain/Pleasure   How can you use these emotions in your motivation?

_____   _____
_____   _____
_____   _____
_____   _____
_____   _____

How will you benefit from achieving this goal?

_____
_____
_____
_____

How might this achievement improve how you feel about yourself?

_____
_____
_____
_____

How will you reward yourself when you've achieved this goal?

_____

_____

_____

_____

_____

Who has already achieved this goal that you may be able to model? _____

Are you willing to research their process and adapt it to your needs? _____

Where else might you find assistance? _____

Who will support you in this process? _____

Rate the following on a scale from 1 – 10 (1 = low and 10 = high) to determine your readiness to achieve this goal and discover areas to work on.

Are you ………………

Committed	_____	Willing to sacrifice	_____	Willing to work now?	_____
Ready	_____	Disciplined	_____	Do you believe it?	_____
Deserving	_____	Consistent	_____	Focused	_____
Dedicated	_____	Capable	_____	Organized	_____
Supported	_____	Confident	_____	Positive	_____

Are you willing to schedule dedicated time to work on this goal daily? _____ If, so how much? _____

List five affirmations you will use to help you achieve this goal.

_____

_____

_____

_____

_____

Accept this goal as already true and write a thank you note to yourself for doing the work and to the universe/god for helping you achieve it.

_____

_____

_____

_____

_____

Describe any positive feelings/emotions you feel around this goal now.

_____

_____

_____

_____

Are you ready to take action towards this goal? _____

If not now, what will help you become ready?

_____

_____

_____

What does success look like?
Doodle, Notes, Images, Brainstorm, Mindmap

Visualize Success

Work

When will you begin working on this?_____

Have you added this goal to your vision board? _____ If not, when will you add it? _____

Where are you today compared to where you want to be with this goal? How can you get there?

Current Status	Goal	Difference/Actions Needed
_____	_____	_____
_____	_____	_____
_____	_____	_____
_____	_____	_____
_____	_____	_____

What skills and resources are already available to you and how can you use them?

Skills/Resources	How can you use it?
_____	_____
_____	_____
_____	_____
_____	_____

What skills and resources do you need and how might you acquire them?

Skills/Resources	How will you acquire it?
_____	_____
_____	_____
_____	_____
_____	_____
_____	_____

List any milestones along this journey.

How will you measure your successes and progress?

_____

_____

How will you hold yourself accountable?

_____

_____

What action will you take today? _____

What daily actions are required (habits)? Identify keystone habits.

Stop	Start	Continue	Increase	Limit

Action Plan

	Steps to Take/Checklist	Timeline
PHASE 1		Start Date:
PHASE 2		
PHASE 3		
PHASE 4		

30-Day Habit Tracker
Goal

Round 1																																
Habit	**Start Date**													**Day**																		
1.		1	2	3	4	5	6	7	8	9	10	11	12	13	14	15	16	17	18	19	20	21	22	23	24	25	26	27	28	29	30
2.		1	2	3	4	5	6	7	8	9	10	11	12	13	14	15	16	17	18	19	20	21	22	23	24	25	26	27	28	29	30
3.		1	2	3	4	5	6	7	8	9	10	11	12	13	14	15	16	17	18	19	20	21	22	23	24	25	26	27	28	29	30
4.		1	2	3	4	5	6	7	8	9	10	11	12	13	14	15	16	17	18	19	20	21	22	23	24	25	26	27	28	29	30
5.		1	2	3	4	5	6	7	8	9	10	11	12	13	14	15	16	17	18	19	20	21	22	23	24	25	26	27	28	29	30

Round 2																																
Habit	**Start Date**													**Day**																		
1.		1	2	3	4	5	6	7	8	9	10	11	12	13	14	15	16	17	18	19	20	21	22	23	24	25	26	27	28	29	30
2.		1	2	3	4	5	6	7	8	9	10	11	12	13	14	15	16	17	18	19	20	21	22	23	24	25	26	27	28	29	30
3.		1	2	3	4	5	6	7	8	9	10	11	12	13	14	15	16	17	18	19	20	21	22	23	24	25	26	27	28	29	30
4.		1	2	3	4	5	6	7	8	9	10	11	12	13	14	15	16	17	18	19	20	21	22	23	24	25	26	27	28	29	30
5.		1	2	3	4	5	6	7	8	9	10	11	12	13	14	15	16	17	18	19	20	21	22	23	24	25	26	27	28	29	30

Round 3																																
Habit	**Start Date**													**Day**																		
1.		1	2	3	4	5	6	7	8	9	10	11	12	13	14	15	16	17	18	19	20	21	22	23	24	25	26	27	28	29	30
2.		1	2	3	4	5	6	7	8	9	10	11	12	13	14	15	16	17	18	19	20	21	22	23	24	25	26	27	28	29	30
3.		1	2	3	4	5	6	7	8	9	10	11	12	13	14	15	16	17	18	19	20	21	22	23	24	25	26	27	28	29	30
4.		1	2	3	4	5	6	7	8	9	10	11	12	13	14	15	16	17	18	19	20	21	22	23	24	25	26	27	28	29	30
5.		1	2	3	4	5	6	7	8	9	10	11	12	13	14	15	16	17	18	19	20	21	22	23	24	25	26	27	28	29	30

Round 4																																
Habit	**Start Date**													**Day**																		
1.		1	2	3	4	5	6	7	8	9	10	11	12	13	14	15	16	17	18	19	20	21	22	23	24	25	26	27	28	29	30
2.		1	2	3	4	5	6	7	8	9	10	11	12	13	14	15	16	17	18	19	20	21	22	23	24	25	26	27	28	29	30
3.		1	2	3	4	5	6	7	8	9	10	11	12	13	14	15	16	17	18	19	20	21	22	23	24	25	26	27	28	29	30
4.		1	2	3	4	5	6	7	8	9	10	11	12	13	14	15	16	17	18	19	20	21	22	23	24	25	26	27	28	29	30
5.		1	2	3	4	5	6	7	8	9	10	11	12	13	14	15	16	17	18	19	20	21	22	23	24	25	26	27	28	29	30

Round 5																																
Habit	**Start Date**													**Day**																		
1.		1	2	3	4	5	6	7	8	9	10	11	12	13	14	15	16	17	18	19	20	21	22	23	24	25	26	27	28	29	30
2.		1	2	3	4	5	6	7	8	9	10	11	12	13	14	15	16	17	18	19	20	21	22	23	24	25	26	27	28	29	30
3.		1	2	3	4	5	6	7	8	9	10	11	12	13	14	15	16	17	18	19	20	21	22	23	24	25	26	27	28	29	30
4.		1	2	3	4	5	6	7	8	9	10	11	12	13	14	15	16	17	18	19	20	21	22	23	24	25	26	27	28	29	30
5.		1	2	3	4	5	6	7	8	9	10	11	12	13	14	15	16	17	18	19	20	21	22	23	24	25	26	27	28	29	30

Round 6																																
Habit	**Start Date**													**Day**																		
1.		1	2	3	4	5	6	7	8	9	10	11	12	13	14	15	16	17	18	19	20	21	22	23	24	25	26	27	28	29	30
2.		1	2	3	4	5	6	7	8	9	10	11	12	13	14	15	16	17	18	19	20	21	22	23	24	25	26	27	28	29	30
3.		1	2	3	4	5	6	7	8	9	10	11	12	13	14	15	16	17	18	19	20	21	22	23	24	25	26	27	28	29	30
4.		1	2	3	4	5	6	7	8	9	10	11	12	13	14	15	16	17	18	19	20	21	22	23	24	25	26	27	28	29	30
5.		1	2	3	4	5	6	7	8	9	10	11	12	13	14	15	16	17	18	19	20	21	22	23	24	25	26	27	28	29	30

Post-Work

Congratulations! You've achieved your goal. Now, celebrate your success. You deserve it!

After the celebration, it's time for evaluation. Take a look back on what you've experienced around this goal. Note any observations, obstacles, and lessons learned and how you apply them in the future.

Was the experience what you expected it to be? If not, why?_____

_____
_____
_____

 What happened with this goal and its execution? Did anything stand out?

_____
_____
_____
_____
_____
_____

Did everything go as planned? _____   Did you stick to the timeline? _____
What went well?

_____
_____
_____
_____

What could've gone better?   How can you make adjustments in the future?

_____   _____
_____   _____
_____   _____
_____   _____

What lessons did you learn?   How will you apply them?

_____   _____
_____   _____
_____   _____
_____   _____

How have you grown from this experience?

_____
_____
_____
_____

How will you maintain this success?

_____
_____
_____
_____

Goal # _____

Pre-Work

Specific	Measurable	Achievable	Realistic/Relevant	Time-bound

Use positive language to rewrite your finalized goal including the SMART elements from above.

_____

_____

What's your motivation? Why do you want to achieve this goal? (Also, do you want to achieve it for yourself or because someone else wants it for you?)

_____
_____
_____
_____
_____

This goals supports objectives: _____

Define this goal. Describe, *in vivid detail*, <u>exactly</u> what you want and what your success looks and feels likes. Use as many senses in the description as possible. Make, model, size, shape, color, year, location, etc.. See, hear, and feel. Use details, details, details!

_____
_____
_____
_____
_____
_____
_____
_____
_____
_____
_____
_____
_____
_____
_____
_____

Success Checklist
Prework
Build SMART Goal
Understand Why
Develop Details
Identify Strengths & Weaknesses
Identify Support
Identify Reward
Assess Commitment
Identify Resources
Identify Changes
Develop Action Plan & Timeline
Work
Visualize & Plant the Seed
Take the 1st Step
Build Affirmation Cards
Track Habits for 30 Days
Execute Plan
Phase 1
Phase 2
Phase 3
Phase 4
Achieve Goal!
Postwork
Celebrate
Evaluate

Have you gotten a clear mental image of this goal? If not what additional details will bring greater clarity?

_____

_____

_____

Can you see yourself achieving this goal? _____

How will you know when you've achieved this goal?

_____

_____

_____

_____

Have you attempted this goal before? _____

What barriers have you encountered in the past and/or what obstacles can you anticipate? How will you overcome them?

Barriers/Obstacles/Fears   How will you overcome them?

_____   _____

_____   _____

_____   _____

_____   _____

_____   _____

What assets and advantages do you have?

Assets/Advantages   How can you use these?

_____   _____

_____   _____

_____   _____

_____   _____

_____   _____

Are there any feelings of pain or pleasure around this goal?

Pain/Pleasure   How can you use these emotions in your motivation?

_____   _____

_____   _____

_____   _____

_____   _____

_____   _____

How will you benefit from achieving this goal?

_____

_____

_____

_____

How might this achievement improve how you feel about yourself?

_____

_____

_____

_____

How will you reward yourself when you've achieved this goal?

_____
_____
_____
_____
_____

Who has already achieved this goal that you may be able to model? _____

Are you willing to research their process and adapt it to your needs? _____

Where else might you find assistance? _____

Who will support you in this process? _____

Rate the following on a scale from 1 – 10 (1 = low and 10 = high) to determine your readiness to achieve this goal and discover areas to work on.

Are you ………………

Committed	_____	Willing to sacrifice	_____	Willing to work now?	_____
Ready	_____	Disciplined	_____	Do you believe it?	_____
Deserving	_____	Consistent	_____	Focused	_____
Dedicated	_____	Capable	_____	Organized	_____
Supported	_____	Confident	_____	Positive	_____

Are you willing to schedule dedicated time to work on this goal daily? _____ If, so how much? _____

List five affirmations you will use to help you achieve this goal.

_____
_____
_____
_____
_____

Accept this goal as already true and write a thank you note to yourself for doing the work and to the universe/god for helping you achieve it.

_____
_____
_____
_____
_____

Describe any positive feelings/emotions you feel around this goal now.

_____
_____
_____
_____

Are you ready to take action towards this goal? _____

If not now, what will help you become ready?

_____
_____
_____

What does success look like?
Doodle, Notes, Images, Brainstorm, Mindmap

Visualize Success

Work

When will you begin working on this?_____

Have you added this goal to your vision board? _____ If not, when will you add it? _____

Where are you today compared to where you want to be with this goal? How can you get there?

Current Status	Goal	Difference/Actions Needed
_____	_____	_____
_____	_____	_____
_____	_____	_____
_____	_____	_____
_____	_____	_____

What skills and resources are already available to you and how can you use them?

Skills/Resources	How can you use it?
_____	_____
_____	_____
_____	_____
_____	_____

What skills and resources do you need and how might you acquire them?

Skills/Resources	How will you acquire it?
_____	_____
_____	_____
_____	_____
_____	_____
_____	_____

List any milestones along this journey.

How will you measure your successes and progress?

_____

How will you hold yourself accountable?

_____

What action will you take today? _____

What daily actions are required (habits)? Identify keystone habits.

Stop	Start	Continue	Increase	Limit

Action Plan

	Steps to Take/Checklist	Timeline
PHASE 1		Start Date:
PHASE 2		
PHASE 3		
PHASE 4		

30-Day Habit Tracker
Goal

Round 1																																
Habit	**Start Date**														**Day**																	
1.		1	2	3	4	5	6	7	8	9	10	11	12	13	14	15	16	17	18	19	20	21	22	23	24	25	26	27	28	29	30
2.		1	2	3	4	5	6	7	8	9	10	11	12	13	14	15	16	17	18	19	20	21	22	23	24	25	26	27	28	29	30
3.		1	2	3	4	5	6	7	8	9	10	11	12	13	14	15	16	17	18	19	20	21	22	23	24	25	26	27	28	29	30
4.		1	2	3	4	5	6	7	8	9	10	11	12	13	14	15	16	17	18	19	20	21	22	23	24	25	26	27	28	29	30
5.		1	2	3	4	5	6	7	8	9	10	11	12	13	14	15	16	17	18	19	20	21	22	23	24	25	26	27	28	29	30

Round 2																																
Habit	**Start Date**														**Day**																	
1.		1	2	3	4	5	6	7	8	9	10	11	12	13	14	15	16	17	18	19	20	21	22	23	24	25	26	27	28	29	30
2.		1	2	3	4	5	6	7	8	9	10	11	12	13	14	15	16	17	18	19	20	21	22	23	24	25	26	27	28	29	30
3.		1	2	3	4	5	6	7	8	9	10	11	12	13	14	15	16	17	18	19	20	21	22	23	24	25	26	27	28	29	30
4.		1	2	3	4	5	6	7	8	9	10	11	12	13	14	15	16	17	18	19	20	21	22	23	24	25	26	27	28	29	30
5.		1	2	3	4	5	6	7	8	9	10	11	12	13	14	15	16	17	18	19	20	21	22	23	24	25	26	27	28	29	30

Round 3																																
Habit	**Start Date**														**Day**																	
1.		1	2	3	4	5	6	7	8	9	10	11	12	13	14	15	16	17	18	19	20	21	22	23	24	25	26	27	28	29	30
2.		1	2	3	4	5	6	7	8	9	10	11	12	13	14	15	16	17	18	19	20	21	22	23	24	25	26	27	28	29	30
3.		1	2	3	4	5	6	7	8	9	10	11	12	13	14	15	16	17	18	19	20	21	22	23	24	25	26	27	28	29	30
4.		1	2	3	4	5	6	7	8	9	10	11	12	13	14	15	16	17	18	19	20	21	22	23	24	25	26	27	28	29	30
5.		1	2	3	4	5	6	7	8	9	10	11	12	13	14	15	16	17	18	19	20	21	22	23	24	25	26	27	28	29	30

Round 4																																
Habit	**Start Date**														**Day**																	
1.		1	2	3	4	5	6	7	8	9	10	11	12	13	14	15	16	17	18	19	20	21	22	23	24	25	26	27	28	29	30
2.		1	2	3	4	5	6	7	8	9	10	11	12	13	14	15	16	17	18	19	20	21	22	23	24	25	26	27	28	29	30
3.		1	2	3	4	5	6	7	8	9	10	11	12	13	14	15	16	17	18	19	20	21	22	23	24	25	26	27	28	29	30
4.		1	2	3	4	5	6	7	8	9	10	11	12	13	14	15	16	17	18	19	20	21	22	23	24	25	26	27	28	29	30
5.		1	2	3	4	5	6	7	8	9	10	11	12	13	14	15	16	17	18	19	20	21	22	23	24	25	26	27	28	29	30

Round 5																																
Habit	**Start Date**														**Day**																	
1.		1	2	3	4	5	6	7	8	9	10	11	12	13	14	15	16	17	18	19	20	21	22	23	24	25	26	27	28	29	30
2.		1	2	3	4	5	6	7	8	9	10	11	12	13	14	15	16	17	18	19	20	21	22	23	24	25	26	27	28	29	30
3.		1	2	3	4	5	6	7	8	9	10	11	12	13	14	15	16	17	18	19	20	21	22	23	24	25	26	27	28	29	30
4.		1	2	3	4	5	6	7	8	9	10	11	12	13	14	15	16	17	18	19	20	21	22	23	24	25	26	27	28	29	30
5.		1	2	3	4	5	6	7	8	9	10	11	12	13	14	15	16	17	18	19	20	21	22	23	24	25	26	27	28	29	30

Round 6																																
Habit	**Start Date**														**Day**																	
1.		1	2	3	4	5	6	7	8	9	10	11	12	13	14	15	16	17	18	19	20	21	22	23	24	25	26	27	28	29	30
2.		1	2	3	4	5	6	7	8	9	10	11	12	13	14	15	16	17	18	19	20	21	22	23	24	25	26	27	28	29	30
3.		1	2	3	4	5	6	7	8	9	10	11	12	13	14	15	16	17	18	19	20	21	22	23	24	25	26	27	28	29	30
4.		1	2	3	4	5	6	7	8	9	10	11	12	13	14	15	16	17	18	19	20	21	22	23	24	25	26	27	28	29	30
5.		1	2	3	4	5	6	7	8	9	10	11	12	13	14	15	16	17	18	19	20	21	22	23	24	25	26	27	28	29	30

Post-Work

Congratulations! You've achieved your goal. Now, celebrate your success. You deserve it!

After the celebration, it's time for evaluation. Take a look back on what you've experienced around this goal. Note any observations, obstacles, and lessons learned and how you apply them in the future.

Was the experience what you expected it to be? If not, why?_____

_____
_____
_____

 What happened with this goal and its execution? Did anything stand out?

_____
_____
_____
_____
_____
_____

Did everything go as planned? _____   Did you stick to the timeline? _____
What went well?

_____
_____
_____
_____

What could've gone better?   How can you make adjustments in the future?

_____   _____
_____   _____
_____   _____
_____   _____

What lessons did you learn?   How will you apply them?

_____   _____
_____   _____
_____   _____
_____   _____

How have you grown from this experience?

_____
_____
_____
_____

How will you maintain this success?

_____
_____
_____
_____

Goal # _____

Pre-Work

Specific	Measurable	Achievable	Realistic/Relevant	Time-bound

Use positive language to rewrite your finalized goal including the SMART elements from above.

_____

_____

What's your motivation? Why do you want to achieve this goal? (Also, do you want to achieve it for yourself or because someone else wants it for you?)

_____

_____

_____

_____

This goals supports objectives: _____

Define this goal. Describe, *in vivid detail*, <u>exactly</u> what you want and what your success looks and feels likes. Use as many senses in the description as possible. Make, model, size, shape, color, year, location, etc.. See, hear, and feel. Use details, details, details!

_____

_____

_____

_____

_____

_____

_____

_____

_____

_____

_____

_____

_____

_____

_____

_____

_____

Success Checklist
Prework
Build SMART Goal
Understand Why
Develop Details
Identify Strengths & Weaknesses
Identify Support
Identify Reward
Assess Commitment
Identify Resources
Identify Changes
Develop Action Plan & Timeline
Work
Visualize & Plant the Seed
Take the 1st Step
Build Affirmation Cards
Track Habits for 30 Days
Execute Plan
Phase 1
Phase 2
Phase 3
Phase 4
Achieve Goal!
Postwork
Celebrate
Evaluate

Have you gotten a clear mental image of this goal? If not what additional details will bring greater clarity?

_____

_____

_____

Can you see yourself achieving this goal? _____

How will you know when you've achieved this goal?

_____

_____

_____

_____

Have you attempted this goal before? _____

What barriers have you encountered in the past and/or what obstacles can you anticipate? How will you overcome them?

Barriers/Obstacles/Fears   How will you overcome them?

_____   _____

_____   _____

_____   _____

_____   _____

_____   _____

What assets and advantages do you have?

Assets/Advantages   How can you use these?

_____   _____

_____   _____

_____   _____

_____   _____

_____   _____

Are there any feelings of pain or pleasure around this goal?

Pain/Pleasure   How can you use these emotions in your motivation?

_____   _____

_____   _____

_____   _____

_____   _____

_____   _____

How will you benefit from achieving this goal?

_____

_____

_____

_____

How might this achievement improve how you feel about yourself?

_____

_____

_____

_____

How will you reward yourself when you've achieved this goal?

_____

_____

_____

_____

_____

Who has already achieved this goal that you may be able to model? _____

Are you willing to research their process and adapt it to your needs? _____

Where else might you find assistance? _____

Who will support you in this process? _____

Rate the following on a scale from 1 – 10 (1 = low and 10 = high) to determine your readiness to achieve this goal and discover areas to work on.

Are you ………………

Committed	_____	Willing to sacrifice	_____	Willing to work now?	_____
Ready	_____	Disciplined	_____	Do you believe it?	_____
Deserving	_____	Consistent	_____	Focused	_____
Dedicated	_____	Capable	_____	Organized	_____
Supported	_____	Confident	_____	Positive	_____

Are you willing to schedule dedicated time to work on this goal daily? _____ If, so how much? _____

List five affirmations you will use to help you achieve this goal.

_____

_____

_____

_____

_____

Accept this goal as already true and write a thank you note to yourself for doing the work and to the universe/god for helping you achieve it.

_____

_____

_____

_____

_____

Describe any positive feelings/emotions you feel around this goal now.

_____

_____

_____

_____

Are you ready to take action towards this goal? _____

If not now, what will help you become ready?

_____

_____

_____

What does success look like?
Doodle, Notes, Images, Brainstorm, Mindmap

Visualize Success

Work

When will you begin working on this?_____

Have you added this goal to your vision board? _____ If not, when will you add it? _____

Where are you today compared to where you want to be with this goal? How can you get there?

Current Status	Goal	Difference/Actions Needed
_____	_____	_____
_____	_____	_____
_____	_____	_____
_____	_____	_____
_____	_____	_____

What skills and resources are already available to you and how can you use them?

Skills/Resources	How can you use it?
_____	_____
_____	_____
_____	_____
_____	_____

What skills and resources do you need and how might you acquire them?

Skills/Resources	How will you acquire it?
_____	_____
_____	_____
_____	_____
_____	_____
_____	_____

List any milestones along this journey.

How will you measure your successes and progress?

_____

How will you hold yourself accountable?

_____

What action will you take today? _____

What daily actions are required (habits)? Identify keystone habits.

Stop	Start	Continue	Increase	Limit

Action Plan

	Steps to Take/Checklist	Timeline
PHASE 1		Start Date:
PHASE 2		
PHASE 3		
PHASE 4		

30-Day Habit Tracker
Goal

Round 1																																	
Habit	**Start Date**																**Day**																	
1.		1	2	3	4	5	6	7	8	9	10	11	12	13	14	15	16	17	18	19	20	21	22	23	24	25	26	27	28	29	30		
2.		1	2	3	4	5	6	7	8	9	10	11	12	13	14	15	16	17	18	19	20	21	22	23	24	25	26	27	28	29	30		
3.		1	2	3	4	5	6	7	8	9	10	11	12	13	14	15	16	17	18	19	20	21	22	23	24	25	26	27	28	29	30		
4.		1	2	3	4	5	6	7	8	9	10	11	12	13	14	15	16	17	18	19	20	21	22	23	24	25	26	27	28	29	30		
5.		1	2	3	4	5	6	7	8	9	10	11	12	13	14	15	16	17	18	19	20	21	22	23	24	25	26	27	28	29	30		

Round 2																																	
Habit	**Start Date**																**Day**																	
1.		1	2	3	4	5	6	7	8	9	10	11	12	13	14	15	16	17	18	19	20	21	22	23	24	25	26	27	28	29	30		
2.		1	2	3	4	5	6	7	8	9	10	11	12	13	14	15	16	17	18	19	20	21	22	23	24	25	26	27	28	29	30		
3.		1	2	3	4	5	6	7	8	9	10	11	12	13	14	15	16	17	18	19	20	21	22	23	24	25	26	27	28	29	30		
4.		1	2	3	4	5	6	7	8	9	10	11	12	13	14	15	16	17	18	19	20	21	22	23	24	25	26	27	28	29	30		
5.		1	2	3	4	5	6	7	8	9	10	11	12	13	14	15	16	17	18	19	20	21	22	23	24	25	26	27	28	29	30		

Round 3																																	
Habit	**Start Date**																**Day**																	
1.		1	2	3	4	5	6	7	8	9	10	11	12	13	14	15	16	17	18	19	20	21	22	23	24	25	26	27	28	29	30		
2.		1	2	3	4	5	6	7	8	9	10	11	12	13	14	15	16	17	18	19	20	21	22	23	24	25	26	27	28	29	30		
3.		1	2	3	4	5	6	7	8	9	10	11	12	13	14	15	16	17	18	19	20	21	22	23	24	25	26	27	28	29	30		
4.		1	2	3	4	5	6	7	8	9	10	11	12	13	14	15	16	17	18	19	20	21	22	23	24	25	26	27	28	29	30		
5.		1	2	3	4	5	6	7	8	9	10	11	12	13	14	15	16	17	18	19	20	21	22	23	24	25	26	27	28	29	30		

Round 4																																	
Habit	**Start Date**																**Day**																	
1.		1	2	3	4	5	6	7	8	9	10	11	12	13	14	15	16	17	18	19	20	21	22	23	24	25	26	27	28	29	30		
2.		1	2	3	4	5	6	7	8	9	10	11	12	13	14	15	16	17	18	19	20	21	22	23	24	25	26	27	28	29	30		
3.		1	2	3	4	5	6	7	8	9	10	11	12	13	14	15	16	17	18	19	20	21	22	23	24	25	26	27	28	29	30		
4.		1	2	3	4	5	6	7	8	9	10	11	12	13	14	15	16	17	18	19	20	21	22	23	24	25	26	27	28	29	30		
5.		1	2	3	4	5	6	7	8	9	10	11	12	13	14	15	16	17	18	19	20	21	22	23	24	25	26	27	28	29	30		

Round 5																																	
Habit	**Start Date**																**Day**																	
1.		1	2	3	4	5	6	7	8	9	10	11	12	13	14	15	16	17	18	19	20	21	22	23	24	25	26	27	28	29	30		
2.		1	2	3	4	5	6	7	8	9	10	11	12	13	14	15	16	17	18	19	20	21	22	23	24	25	26	27	28	29	30		
3.		1	2	3	4	5	6	7	8	9	10	11	12	13	14	15	16	17	18	19	20	21	22	23	24	25	26	27	28	29	30		
4.		1	2	3	4	5	6	7	8	9	10	11	12	13	14	15	16	17	18	19	20	21	22	23	24	25	26	27	28	29	30		
5.		1	2	3	4	5	6	7	8	9	10	11	12	13	14	15	16	17	18	19	20	21	22	23	24	25	26	27	28	29	30		

Round 6																																	
Habit	**Start Date**																**Day**																	
1.		1	2	3	4	5	6	7	8	9	10	11	12	13	14	15	16	17	18	19	20	21	22	23	24	25	26	27	28	29	30		
2.		1	2	3	4	5	6	7	8	9	10	11	12	13	14	15	16	17	18	19	20	21	22	23	24	25	26	27	28	29	30		
3.		1	2	3	4	5	6	7	8	9	10	11	12	13	14	15	16	17	18	19	20	21	22	23	24	25	26	27	28	29	30		
4.		1	2	3	4	5	6	7	8	9	10	11	12	13	14	15	16	17	18	19	20	21	22	23	24	25	26	27	28	29	30		
5.		1	2	3	4	5	6	7	8	9	10	11	12	13	14	15	16	17	18	19	20	21	22	23	24	25	26	27	28	29	30		

Post-Work

Congratulations! You've achieved your goal. Now, celebrate your success. You deserve it!

After the celebration, it's time for evaluation. Take a look back on what you've experienced around this goal. Note any observations, obstacles, and lessons learned and how you apply them in the future.

Was the experience what you expected it to be? If not, why?_____

_____
_____
_____

 What happened with this goal and its execution? Did anything stand out?

_____
_____
_____
_____
_____
_____

Did everything go as planned? _____   Did you stick to the timeline? _____
What went well?

_____
_____
_____
_____

What could've gone better?   How can you make adjustments in the future?

_____   _____
_____   _____
_____   _____
_____   _____

What lessons did you learn?   How will you apply them?

_____   _____
_____   _____
_____   _____
_____   _____

How have you grown from this experience?

_____
_____
_____
_____

How will you maintain this success?

_____
_____
_____
_____

Goal # _____

☐ _____
Date Completed

Pre-Work

Specific	Measurable	Achievable	Realistic/Relevant	Time-bound

Use positive language to rewrite your finalized goal including the SMART elements from above.

_____

_____

What's your motivation? Why do you want to achieve this goal? (Also, do you want to achieve it for yourself or because someone else wants it for you?)

_____

_____

_____

_____

This goals supports objectives: _____

Define this goal. Describe, *in vivid detail*, <u>exactly</u> what you want and what your success looks and feels likes. Use as many senses in the description as possible. Make, model, size, shape, color, year, location, etc.. See, hear, and feel. Use details, details, details!

_____

_____

_____

_____

_____

_____

_____

_____

_____

_____

_____

_____

_____

_____

_____

Success Checklist
Prework
Build SMART Goal
Understand Why
Develop Details
Identify Strengths & Weaknesses
Identify Support
Identify Reward
Assess Commitment
Identify Resources
Identify Changes
Develop Action Plan & Timeline
Work
Visualize & Plant the Seed
Take the 1st Step
Build Affirmation Cards
Track Habits for 30 Days
Execute Plan
Phase 1
Phase 2
Phase 3
Phase 4
Achieve Goal!
Postwork
Celebrate
Evaluate

Have you gotten a clear mental image of this goal? If not what additional details will bring greater clarity?

_____

_____

_____

Can you see yourself achieving this goal? _____

How will you know when you've achieved this goal?

_____

_____

_____

_____

Have you attempted this goal before? _____

What barriers have you encountered in the past and/or what obstacles can you anticipate? How will you overcome them?

Barriers/Obstacles/Fears	How will you overcome them?
_____	_____
_____	_____
_____	_____
_____	_____
_____	_____

What assets and advantages do you have?

Assets/Advantages	How can you use these?
_____	_____
_____	_____
_____	_____
_____	_____
_____	_____

Are there any feelings of pain or pleasure around this goal?

Pain/Pleasure	How can you use these emotions in your motivation?
_____	_____
_____	_____
_____	_____
_____	_____
_____	_____

How will you benefit from achieving this goal?

_____

_____

_____

_____

How might this achievement improve how you feel about yourself?

_____

_____

_____

_____

How will you reward yourself when you've achieved this goal?

_____
_____
_____
_____
_____

Who has already achieved this goal that you may be able to model? _____

Are you willing to research their process and adapt it to your needs? _____

Where else might you find assistance? _____

Who will support you in this process? _____

Rate the following on a scale from 1 – 10 (1 = low and 10 = high) to determine your readiness to achieve this goal and discover areas to work on.

Are you ………………..

Committed	_____	Willing to sacrifice	_____	Willing to work now?	_____
Ready	_____	Disciplined	_____	Do you believe it?	_____
Deserving	_____	Consistent	_____	Focused	_____
Dedicated	_____	Capable	_____	Organized	_____
Supported	_____	Confident	_____	Positive	_____

Are you willing to schedule dedicated time to work on this goal daily? _____ If, so how much? _____

List five affirmations you will use to help you achieve this goal.

_____
_____
_____
_____
_____

Accept this goal as already true and write a thank you note to yourself for doing the work and to the universe/god for helping you achieve it.

_____
_____
_____
_____
_____

Describe any positive feelings/emotions you feel around this goal now.

_____
_____
_____
_____

Are you ready to take action towards this goal? _____

If not now, what will help you become ready?

_____
_____
_____

What does success look like?
Doodle, Notes, Images, Brainstorm, Mindmap

Visualize Success

Work

When will you begin working on this?_____

Have you added this goal to your vision board? _____ If not, when will you add it? _____

Where are you today compared to where you want to be with this goal? How can you get there?

Current Status	Goal	Difference/Actions Needed
_____	_____	_____
_____	_____	_____
_____	_____	_____
_____	_____	_____
_____	_____	_____

What skills and resources are already available to you and how can you use them?

Skills/Resources   How can you use it?

What skills and resources do you need and how might you acquire them?

Skills/Resources   How will you acquire it?

List any milestones along this journey.   How will you measure your successes and progress?

How will you hold yourself accountable?

What action will you take today? _____

What daily actions are required (habits)? Identify keystone habits.

Stop	Start	Continue	Increase	Limit

Action Plan

	Steps to Take/Checklist	Timeline
PHASE 1		Start Date:
PHASE 2		
PHASE 3		
PHASE 4		

30-Day Habit Tracker
Goal

Round 1																																
Habit	**Start Date**																	**Day**														
1.		1	2	3	4	5	6	7	8	9	10	11	12	13	14	15	16	17	18	19	20	21	22	23	24	25	26	27	28	29	30
2.		1	2	3	4	5	6	7	8	9	10	11	12	13	14	15	16	17	18	19	20	21	22	23	24	25	26	27	28	29	30
3.		1	2	3	4	5	6	7	8	9	10	11	12	13	14	15	16	17	18	19	20	21	22	23	24	25	26	27	28	29	30
4.		1	2	3	4	5	6	7	8	9	10	11	12	13	14	15	16	17	18	19	20	21	22	23	24	25	26	27	28	29	30
5.		1	2	3	4	5	6	7	8	9	10	11	12	13	14	15	16	17	18	19	20	21	22	23	24	25	26	27	28	29	30

Round 2																																
Habit	**Start Date**																	**Day**														
1.		1	2	3	4	5	6	7	8	9	10	11	12	13	14	15	16	17	18	19	20	21	22	23	24	25	26	27	28	29	30
2.		1	2	3	4	5	6	7	8	9	10	11	12	13	14	15	16	17	18	19	20	21	22	23	24	25	26	27	28	29	30
3.		1	2	3	4	5	6	7	8	9	10	11	12	13	14	15	16	17	18	19	20	21	22	23	24	25	26	27	28	29	30
4.		1	2	3	4	5	6	7	8	9	10	11	12	13	14	15	16	17	18	19	20	21	22	23	24	25	26	27	28	29	30
5.		1	2	3	4	5	6	7	8	9	10	11	12	13	14	15	16	17	18	19	20	21	22	23	24	25	26	27	28	29	30

Round 3																																
Habit	**Start Date**																	**Day**														
1.		1	2	3	4	5	6	7	8	9	10	11	12	13	14	15	16	17	18	19	20	21	22	23	24	25	26	27	28	29	30
2.		1	2	3	4	5	6	7	8	9	10	11	12	13	14	15	16	17	18	19	20	21	22	23	24	25	26	27	28	29	30
3.		1	2	3	4	5	6	7	8	9	10	11	12	13	14	15	16	17	18	19	20	21	22	23	24	25	26	27	28	29	30
4.		1	2	3	4	5	6	7	8	9	10	11	12	13	14	15	16	17	18	19	20	21	22	23	24	25	26	27	28	29	30
5.		1	2	3	4	5	6	7	8	9	10	11	12	13	14	15	16	17	18	19	20	21	22	23	24	25	26	27	28	29	30

Round 4																																
Habit	**Start Date**																	**Day**														
1.		1	2	3	4	5	6	7	8	9	10	11	12	13	14	15	16	17	18	19	20	21	22	23	24	25	26	27	28	29	30
2.		1	2	3	4	5	6	7	8	9	10	11	12	13	14	15	16	17	18	19	20	21	22	23	24	25	26	27	28	29	30
3.		1	2	3	4	5	6	7	8	9	10	11	12	13	14	15	16	17	18	19	20	21	22	23	24	25	26	27	28	29	30
4.		1	2	3	4	5	6	7	8	9	10	11	12	13	14	15	16	17	18	19	20	21	22	23	24	25	26	27	28	29	30
5.		1	2	3	4	5	6	7	8	9	10	11	12	13	14	15	16	17	18	19	20	21	22	23	24	25	26	27	28	29	30

Round 5																																
Habit	**Start Date**																	**Day**														
1.		1	2	3	4	5	6	7	8	9	10	11	12	13	14	15	16	17	18	19	20	21	22	23	24	25	26	27	28	29	30
2.		1	2	3	4	5	6	7	8	9	10	11	12	13	14	15	16	17	18	19	20	21	22	23	24	25	26	27	28	29	30
3.		1	2	3	4	5	6	7	8	9	10	11	12	13	14	15	16	17	18	19	20	21	22	23	24	25	26	27	28	29	30
4.		1	2	3	4	5	6	7	8	9	10	11	12	13	14	15	16	17	18	19	20	21	22	23	24	25	26	27	28	29	30
5.		1	2	3	4	5	6	7	8	9	10	11	12	13	14	15	16	17	18	19	20	21	22	23	24	25	26	27	28	29	30

Round 6																																
Habit	**Start Date**																	**Day**														
1.		1	2	3	4	5	6	7	8	9	10	11	12	13	14	15	16	17	18	19	20	21	22	23	24	25	26	27	28	29	30
2.		1	2	3	4	5	6	7	8	9	10	11	12	13	14	15	16	17	18	19	20	21	22	23	24	25	26	27	28	29	30
3.		1	2	3	4	5	6	7	8	9	10	11	12	13	14	15	16	17	18	19	20	21	22	23	24	25	26	27	28	29	30
4.		1	2	3	4	5	6	7	8	9	10	11	12	13	14	15	16	17	18	19	20	21	22	23	24	25	26	27	28	29	30
5.		1	2	3	4	5	6	7	8	9	10	11	12	13	14	15	16	17	18	19	20	21	22	23	24	25	26	27	28	29	30

Post-Work

Congratulations! You've achieved your goal. Now, celebrate your success. You deserve it!

After the celebration, it's time for evaluation. Take a look back on what you've experienced around this goal. Note any observations, obstacles, and lessons learned and how you apply them in the future.

Was the experience what you expected it to be? If not, why?_____

_____
_____
_____

What happened with this goal and its execution? Did anything stand out?

_____
_____
_____
_____
_____
_____

Did everything go as planned? _____   Did you stick to the timeline? _____
What went well?

_____
_____
_____
_____

What could've gone better?   How can you make adjustments in the future?

_____   _____
_____   _____
_____   _____
_____   _____

What lessons did you learn?   How will you apply them?

_____   _____
_____   _____
_____   _____
_____   _____

How have you grown from this experience?

_____
_____
_____

How will you maintain this success?

_____
_____
_____
_____

Goal # _____

Pre-Work

Specific	Measurable	Achievable	Realistic/Relevant	Time-bound

Use positive language to rewrite your finalized goal including the SMART elements from above.

_____

_____

What's your motivation? Why do you want to achieve this goal? (Also, do you want to achieve it for yourself or because someone else wants it for you?)

_____

_____

_____

_____

This goals supports objectives: _____

Define this goal. Describe, *in vivid detail*, <u>exactly</u> what you want and what your success looks and feels likes. Use as many senses in the description as possible. Make, model, size, shape, color, year, location, etc.. See, hear, and feel. Use details, details, details!

_____

_____

_____

_____

_____

_____

_____

_____

_____

_____

_____

_____

_____

_____

_____

_____

Success Checklist
Prework
Build SMART Goal
Understand Why
Develop Details
Identify Strengths & Weaknesses
Identify Support
Identify Reward
Assess Commitment
Identify Resources
Identify Changes
Develop Action Plan & Timeline
Work
Visualize & Plant the Seed
Take the 1st Step
Build Affirmation Cards
Track Habits for 30 Days
Execute Plan
Phase 1
Phase 2
Phase 3
Phase 4
Achieve Goal!
Postwork
Celebrate
Evaluate

Have you gotten a clear mental image of this goal? If not what additional details will bring greater clarity?

_____
_____
_____

Can you see yourself achieving this goal? _____

How will you know when you've achieved this goal?

_____
_____
_____
_____

Have you attempted this goal before? _____

What barriers have you encountered in the past and/or what obstacles can you anticipate? How will you overcome them?

Barriers/Obstacles/Fears	How will you overcome them?
_____	_____
_____	_____
_____	_____
_____	_____
_____	_____

What assets and advantages do you have?

Assets/Advantages	How can you use these?
_____	_____
_____	_____
_____	_____
_____	_____
_____	_____

Are there any feelings of pain or pleasure around this goal?

Pain/Pleasure	How can you use these emotions in your motivation?
_____	_____
_____	_____
_____	_____
_____	_____
_____	_____

How will you benefit from achieving this goal?

_____
_____
_____
_____

How might this achievement improve how you feel about yourself?

_____
_____
_____
_____

How will you reward yourself when you've achieved this goal?

_____
_____
_____
_____
_____

Who has already achieved this goal that you may be able to model? _____

Are you willing to research their process and adapt it to your needs? _____

Where else might you find assistance? _____

Who will support you in this process? _____

Rate the following on a scale from 1 – 10 (1 = low and 10 = high) to determine your readiness to achieve this goal and discover areas to work on.

Are you ………………

Committed	_____	Willing to sacrifice	_____	Willing to work now?	_____
Ready	_____	Disciplined	_____	Do you believe it?	_____
Deserving	_____	Consistent	_____	Focused	_____
Dedicated	_____	Capable	_____	Organized	_____
Supported	_____	Confident	_____	Positive	_____

Are you willing to schedule dedicated time to work on this goal daily? _____ If, so how much? _____

List five affirmations you will use to help you achieve this goal.

_____
_____
_____
_____
_____

Accept this goal as already true and write a thank you note to yourself for doing the work and to the universe/god for helping you achieve it.

_____
_____
_____
_____
_____

Describe any positive feelings/emotions you feel around this goal now.

_____
_____
_____
_____

Are you ready to take action towards this goal? _____

If not now, what will help you become ready?

_____
_____
_____

What does success look like?
Doodle, Notes, Images, Brainstorm, Mindmap

Visualize Success

Work

When will you begin working on this?_____

Have you added this goal to your vision board? _____ If not, when will you add it? _____

Where are you today compared to where you want to be with this goal? How can you get there?

Current Status	Goal	Difference/Actions Needed
_____	_____	_____
_____	_____	_____
_____	_____	_____
_____	_____	_____
_____	_____	_____

What skills and resources are already available to you and how can you use them?

Skills/Resources   How can you use it?

_____   _____
_____   _____
_____   _____
_____   _____

What skills and resources do you need and how might you acquire them?

Skills/Resources   How will you acquire it?

_____   _____
_____   _____
_____   _____
_____   _____

List any milestones along this journey.   How will you measure your successes and progress?

_____   _____
_____   _____
_____   How will you hold yourself accountable?
_____   _____
_____   _____

What action will you take today? _____

What daily actions are required (habits)? Identify keystone habits.

Stop	Start	Continue	Increase	Limit

Action Plan

	Steps to Take/Checklist	Timeline
PHASE 1		Start Date:
PHASE 2		
PHASE 3		
PHASE 4		

30-Day Habit Tracker
Goal

Round 1

Habit	Start Date	Day
1.		1 2 3 4 5 6 7 8 9 10 11 12 13 14 15 16 17 18 19 20 21 22 23 24 25 26 27 28 29 30
2.		1 2 3 4 5 6 7 8 9 10 11 12 13 14 15 16 17 18 19 20 21 22 23 24 25 26 27 28 29 30
3.		1 2 3 4 5 6 7 8 9 10 11 12 13 14 15 16 17 18 19 20 21 22 23 24 25 26 27 28 29 30
4.		1 2 3 4 5 6 7 8 9 10 11 12 13 14 15 16 17 18 19 20 21 22 23 24 25 26 27 28 29 30
5.		1 2 3 4 5 6 7 8 9 10 11 12 13 14 15 16 17 18 19 20 21 22 23 24 25 26 27 28 29 30

Round 2

Habit	Start Date	Day
1.		1 2 3 4 5 6 7 8 9 10 11 12 13 14 15 16 17 18 19 20 21 22 23 24 25 26 27 28 29 30
2.		1 2 3 4 5 6 7 8 9 10 11 12 13 14 15 16 17 18 19 20 21 22 23 24 25 26 27 28 29 30
3.		1 2 3 4 5 6 7 8 9 10 11 12 13 14 15 16 17 18 19 20 21 22 23 24 25 26 27 28 29 30
4.		1 2 3 4 5 6 7 8 9 10 11 12 13 14 15 16 17 18 19 20 21 22 23 24 25 26 27 28 29 30
5.		1 2 3 4 5 6 7 8 9 10 11 12 13 14 15 16 17 18 19 20 21 22 23 24 25 26 27 28 29 30

Round 3

Habit	Start Date	Day
1.		1 2 3 4 5 6 7 8 9 10 11 12 13 14 15 16 17 18 19 20 21 22 23 24 25 26 27 28 29 30
2.		1 2 3 4 5 6 7 8 9 10 11 12 13 14 15 16 17 18 19 20 21 22 23 24 25 26 27 28 29 30
3.		1 2 3 4 5 6 7 8 9 10 11 12 13 14 15 16 17 18 19 20 21 22 23 24 25 26 27 28 29 30
4.		1 2 3 4 5 6 7 8 9 10 11 12 13 14 15 16 17 18 19 20 21 22 23 24 25 26 27 28 29 30
5.		1 2 3 4 5 6 7 8 9 10 11 12 13 14 15 16 17 18 19 20 21 22 23 24 25 26 27 28 29 30

Round 4

Habit	Start Date	Day
1.		1 2 3 4 5 6 7 8 9 10 11 12 13 14 15 16 17 18 19 20 21 22 23 24 25 26 27 28 29 30
2.		1 2 3 4 5 6 7 8 9 10 11 12 13 14 15 16 17 18 19 20 21 22 23 24 25 26 27 28 29 30
3.		1 2 3 4 5 6 7 8 9 10 11 12 13 14 15 16 17 18 19 20 21 22 23 24 25 26 27 28 29 30
4.		1 2 3 4 5 6 7 8 9 10 11 12 13 14 15 16 17 18 19 20 21 22 23 24 25 26 27 28 29 30
5.		1 2 3 4 5 6 7 8 9 10 11 12 13 14 15 16 17 18 19 20 21 22 23 24 25 26 27 28 29 30

Round 5

Habit	Start Date	Day
1.		1 2 3 4 5 6 7 8 9 10 11 12 13 14 15 16 17 18 19 20 21 22 23 24 25 26 27 28 29 30
2.		1 2 3 4 5 6 7 8 9 10 11 12 13 14 15 16 17 18 19 20 21 22 23 24 25 26 27 28 29 30
3.		1 2 3 4 5 6 7 8 9 10 11 12 13 14 15 16 17 18 19 20 21 22 23 24 25 26 27 28 29 30
4.		1 2 3 4 5 6 7 8 9 10 11 12 13 14 15 16 17 18 19 20 21 22 23 24 25 26 27 28 29 30
5.		1 2 3 4 5 6 7 8 9 10 11 12 13 14 15 16 17 18 19 20 21 22 23 24 25 26 27 28 29 30

Round 6

Habit	Start Date	Day
1.		1 2 3 4 5 6 7 8 9 10 11 12 13 14 15 16 17 18 19 20 21 22 23 24 25 26 27 28 29 30
2.		1 2 3 4 5 6 7 8 9 10 11 12 13 14 15 16 17 18 19 20 21 22 23 24 25 26 27 28 29 30
3.		1 2 3 4 5 6 7 8 9 10 11 12 13 14 15 16 17 18 19 20 21 22 23 24 25 26 27 28 29 30
4.		1 2 3 4 5 6 7 8 9 10 11 12 13 14 15 16 17 18 19 20 21 22 23 24 25 26 27 28 29 30
5.		1 2 3 4 5 6 7 8 9 10 11 12 13 14 15 16 17 18 19 20 21 22 23 24 25 26 27 28 29 30

Post-Work

Congratulations! You've achieved your goal. Now, celebrate your success. You deserve it!

After the celebration, it's time for evaluation. Take a look back on what you've experienced around this goal. Note any observations, obstacles, and lessons learned and how you apply them in the future.

Was the experience what you expected it to be? If not, why?_____

_____
_____
_____

What happened with this goal and its execution? Did anything stand out?

_____
_____
_____
_____
_____
_____

Did everything go as planned? _____   Did you stick to the timeline? _____
What went well?

_____
_____
_____
_____

What could've gone better?   How can you make adjustments in the future?

_____   _____
_____   _____
_____   _____
_____   _____

What lessons did you learn?   How will you apply them?

_____   _____
_____   _____
_____   _____
_____   _____

How have you grown from this experience?

_____
_____
_____

How will you maintain this success?

_____
_____
_____
_____

Goal # _____

Pre-Work

Specific	Measurable	Achievable	Realistic/Relevant	Time-bound

Use positive language to rewrite your finalized goal including the SMART elements from above.

_____

_____

What's your motivation? Why do you want to achieve this goal? (Also, do you want to achieve it for yourself or because someone else wants it for you?)

_____

_____

_____

_____

This goals supports objectives: _____

Define this goal. Describe, *in vivid detail*, exactly what you want and what your success looks and feels likes. Use as many senses in the description as possible. Make, model, size, shape, color, year, location, etc.. See, hear, and feel. Use details, details, details!

_____

_____

_____

_____

_____

_____

_____

_____

_____

_____

_____

_____

_____

_____

Success Checklist	
Prework	
	Build SMART Goal
	Understand Why
	Develop Details
	Identify Strengths & Weaknesses
	Identify Support
	Identify Reward
	Assess Commitment
	Identify Resources
	Identify Changes
	Develop Action Plan & Timeline
Work	
	Visualize & Plant the Seed
	Take the 1st Step
	Build Affirmation Cards
	Track Habits for 30 Days
Execute Plan	
	Phase 1
	Phase 2
	Phase 3
	Phase 4
	Achieve Goal!
Postwork	
	Celebrate
	Evaluate

Have you gotten a clear mental image of this goal? If not what additional details will bring greater clarity?

_____
_____
_____

Can you see yourself achieving this goal? _____

How will you know when you've achieved this goal?

_____
_____
_____
_____

Have you attempted this goal before? _____

What barriers have you encountered in the past and/or what obstacles can you anticipate? How will you overcome them?

Barriers/Obstacles/Fears   How will you overcome them?

_____   _____
_____   _____
_____   _____
_____   _____
_____   _____

What assets and advantages do you have?

Assets/Advantages   How can you use these?

_____   _____
_____   _____
_____   _____
_____   _____
_____   _____

Are there any feelings of pain or pleasure around this goal?

Pain/Pleasure   How can you use these emotions in your motivation?

_____   _____
_____   _____
_____   _____
_____   _____
_____   _____

How will you benefit from achieving this goal?

_____
_____
_____
_____

How might this achievement improve how you feel about yourself?

_____
_____
_____
_____

How will you reward yourself when you've achieved this goal?

_____

_____

_____

_____

_____

Who has already achieved this goal that you may be able to model? _____

Are you willing to research their process and adapt it to your needs? _____

Where else might you find assistance? _____

Who will support you in this process? _____

Rate the following on a scale from 1 – 10 (1 = low and 10 = high) to determine your readiness to achieve this goal and discover areas to work on.

Are you ………………

Committed	_____	Willing to sacrifice	_____	Willing to work now?	_____
Ready	_____	Disciplined	_____	Do you believe it?	_____
Deserving	_____	Consistent	_____	Focused	_____
Dedicated	_____	Capable	_____	Organized	_____
Supported	_____	Confident	_____	Positive	_____

Are you willing to schedule dedicated time to work on this goal daily? _____ If, so how much? _____

List five affirmations you will use to help you achieve this goal.

_____

_____

_____

_____

_____

Accept this goal as already true and write a thank you note to yourself for doing the work and to the universe/god for helping you achieve it.

_____

_____

_____

_____

_____

Describe any positive feelings/emotions you feel around this goal now.

_____

_____

_____

_____

Are you ready to take action towards this goal? _____

If not now, what will help you become ready?

_____

_____

_____

What does success look like?
Doodle, Notes, Images, Brainstorm, Mindmap

Visualize Success

Work

When will you begin working on this?_____

Have you added this goal to your vision board? _____ If not, when will you add it? _____

Where are you today compared to where you want to be with this goal? How can you get there?

Current Status	Goal	Difference/Actions Needed
_____	_____	_____
_____	_____	_____
_____	_____	_____
_____	_____	_____
_____	_____	_____

What skills and resources are already available to you and how can you use them?

Skills/Resources   How can you use it?

_____   _____

_____   _____

_____   _____

_____   _____

What skills and resources do you need and how might you acquire them?

Skills/Resources   How will you acquire it?

_____   _____

_____   _____

_____   _____

_____   _____

_____   _____

List any milestones along this journey.   How will you measure your successes and progress?

_____   _____

_____   _____

_____   How will you hold yourself accountable?

_____   _____

_____   _____

What action will you take today? _____

What daily actions are required (habits)? Identify keystone habits.

Stop	Start	Continue	Increase	Limit

Action Plan

	Steps to Take/Checklist	Timeline
PHASE 1		Start Date:
PHASE 2		
PHASE 3		
PHASE 4		

30-Day Habit Tracker
Goal

Round 1		

Habit	Start Date	Day
1.		1 2 3 4 5 6 7 8 9 10 11 12 13 14 15 16 17 18 19 20 21 22 23 24 25 26 27 28 29 30
2.		1 2 3 4 5 6 7 8 9 10 11 12 13 14 15 16 17 18 19 20 21 22 23 24 25 26 27 28 29 30
3.		1 2 3 4 5 6 7 8 9 10 11 12 13 14 15 16 17 18 19 20 21 22 23 24 25 26 27 28 29 30
4.		1 2 3 4 5 6 7 8 9 10 11 12 13 14 15 16 17 18 19 20 21 22 23 24 25 26 27 28 29 30
5.		1 2 3 4 5 6 7 8 9 10 11 12 13 14 15 16 17 18 19 20 21 22 23 24 25 26 27 28 29 30

Round 2		

Habit	Start Date	Day
1.		1 2 3 4 5 6 7 8 9 10 11 12 13 14 15 16 17 18 19 20 21 22 23 24 25 26 27 28 29 30
2.		1 2 3 4 5 6 7 8 9 10 11 12 13 14 15 16 17 18 19 20 21 22 23 24 25 26 27 28 29 30
3.		1 2 3 4 5 6 7 8 9 10 11 12 13 14 15 16 17 18 19 20 21 22 23 24 25 26 27 28 29 30
4.		1 2 3 4 5 6 7 8 9 10 11 12 13 14 15 16 17 18 19 20 21 22 23 24 25 26 27 28 29 30
5.		1 2 3 4 5 6 7 8 9 10 11 12 13 14 15 16 17 18 19 20 21 22 23 24 25 26 27 28 29 30

Round 3		

Habit	Start Date	Day
1.		1 2 3 4 5 6 7 8 9 10 11 12 13 14 15 16 17 18 19 20 21 22 23 24 25 26 27 28 29 30
2.		1 2 3 4 5 6 7 8 9 10 11 12 13 14 15 16 17 18 19 20 21 22 23 24 25 26 27 28 29 30
3.		1 2 3 4 5 6 7 8 9 10 11 12 13 14 15 16 17 18 19 20 21 22 23 24 25 26 27 28 29 30
4.		1 2 3 4 5 6 7 8 9 10 11 12 13 14 15 16 17 18 19 20 21 22 23 24 25 26 27 28 29 30
5.		1 2 3 4 5 6 7 8 9 10 11 12 13 14 15 16 17 18 19 20 21 22 23 24 25 26 27 28 29 30

Round 4		

Habit	Start Date	Day
1.		1 2 3 4 5 6 7 8 9 10 11 12 13 14 15 16 17 18 19 20 21 22 23 24 25 26 27 28 29 30
2.		1 2 3 4 5 6 7 8 9 10 11 12 13 14 15 16 17 18 19 20 21 22 23 24 25 26 27 28 29 30
3.		1 2 3 4 5 6 7 8 9 10 11 12 13 14 15 16 17 18 19 20 21 22 23 24 25 26 27 28 29 30
4.		1 2 3 4 5 6 7 8 9 10 11 12 13 14 15 16 17 18 19 20 21 22 23 24 25 26 27 28 29 30
5.		1 2 3 4 5 6 7 8 9 10 11 12 13 14 15 16 17 18 19 20 21 22 23 24 25 26 27 28 29 30

Round 5		

Habit	Start Date	Day
1.		1 2 3 4 5 6 7 8 9 10 11 12 13 14 15 16 17 18 19 20 21 22 23 24 25 26 27 28 29 30
2.		1 2 3 4 5 6 7 8 9 10 11 12 13 14 15 16 17 18 19 20 21 22 23 24 25 26 27 28 29 30
3.		1 2 3 4 5 6 7 8 9 10 11 12 13 14 15 16 17 18 19 20 21 22 23 24 25 26 27 28 29 30
4.		1 2 3 4 5 6 7 8 9 10 11 12 13 14 15 16 17 18 19 20 21 22 23 24 25 26 27 28 29 30
5.		1 2 3 4 5 6 7 8 9 10 11 12 13 14 15 16 17 18 19 20 21 22 23 24 25 26 27 28 29 30

Round 6		

Habit	Start Date	Day
1.		1 2 3 4 5 6 7 8 9 10 11 12 13 14 15 16 17 18 19 20 21 22 23 24 25 26 27 28 29 30
2.		1 2 3 4 5 6 7 8 9 10 11 12 13 14 15 16 17 18 19 20 21 22 23 24 25 26 27 28 29 30
3.		1 2 3 4 5 6 7 8 9 10 11 12 13 14 15 16 17 18 19 20 21 22 23 24 25 26 27 28 29 30
4.		1 2 3 4 5 6 7 8 9 10 11 12 13 14 15 16 17 18 19 20 21 22 23 24 25 26 27 28 29 30
5.		1 2 3 4 5 6 7 8 9 10 11 12 13 14 15 16 17 18 19 20 21 22 23 24 25 26 27 28 29 30

Post-Work

Congratulations! You've achieved your goal. Now, celebrate your success. You deserve it!

After the celebration, it's time for evaluation. Take a look back on what you've experienced around this goal. Note any observations, obstacles, and lessons learned and how you apply them in the future.

Was the experience what you expected it to be? If not, why?_____

_____

_____

_____

 What happened with this goal and its execution? Did anything stand out?

_____

_____

_____

_____

_____

_____

Did everything go as planned? _____   Did you stick to the timeline? _____
What went well?

_____

_____

_____

_____

What could've gone better?   How can you make adjustments in the future?

_____   _____

_____   _____

_____   _____

_____   _____

What lessons did you learn?   How will you apply them?

_____   _____

_____   _____

_____   _____

_____   _____

How have you grown from this experience?

_____

_____

_____

How will you maintain this success?

_____

_____

_____

_____

Goal # _____

Pre-Work

Specific	Measurable	Achievable	Realistic/Relevant	Time-bound

Use positive language to rewrite your finalized goal including the SMART elements from above.

_____

_____

What's your motivation? Why do you want to achieve this goal? (Also, do you want to achieve it for yourself or because someone else wants it for you?)

_____

_____

_____

_____

This goals supports objectives: _____

Define this goal. Describe, *in vivid detail*, exactly what you want and what your success looks and feels likes. Use as many senses in the description as possible. Make, model, size, shape, color, year, location, etc.. See, hear, and feel. Use details, details, details!

_____

_____

_____

_____

_____

_____

_____

_____

_____

_____

_____

_____

_____

_____

_____

Success Checklist
Prework
Build SMART Goal
Understand Why
Develop Details
Identify Strengths & Weaknesses
Identify Support
Identify Reward
Assess Commitment
Identify Resources
Identify Changes
Develop Action Plan & Timeline
Work
Visualize & Plant the Seed
Take the 1st Step
Build Affirmation Cards
Track Habits for 30 Days
Execute Plan
Phase 1
Phase 2
Phase 3
Phase 4
Achieve Goal!
Postwork
Celebrate
Evaluate

Have you gotten a clear mental image of this goal? If not what additional details will bring greater clarity?

_____
_____
_____

Can you see yourself achieving this goal? _____

How will you know when you've achieved this goal?

_____
_____
_____
_____

Have you attempted this goal before? _____

What barriers have you encountered in the past and/or what obstacles can you anticipate? How will you overcome them?

Barriers/Obstacles/Fears	How will you overcome them?
_____	_____
_____	_____
_____	_____
_____	_____
_____	

What assets and advantages do you have?

Assets/Advantages	How can you use these?
_____	_____
_____	_____
_____	_____
_____	_____

Are there any feelings of pain or pleasure around this goal?

Pain/Pleasure	How can you use these emotions in your motivation?
_____	_____
_____	_____
_____	_____
_____	_____

How will you benefit from achieving this goal?

_____
_____
_____
_____

How might this achievement improve how you feel about yourself?

_____
_____
_____
_____

How will you reward yourself when you've achieved this goal?

_____

_____

_____

_____

_____

Who has already achieved this goal that you may be able to model? _____

Are you willing to research their process and adapt it to your needs? _____

Where else might you find assistance? _____

Who will support you in this process? _____

Rate the following on a scale from 1 – 10 (1 = low and 10 = high) to determine your readiness to achieve this goal and discover areas to work on.

Are you ……………….

Committed	_____	Willing to sacrifice	_____	Willing to work now?	_____
Ready	_____	Disciplined	_____	Do you believe it?	_____
Deserving	_____	Consistent	_____	Focused	_____
Dedicated	_____	Capable	_____	Organized	_____
Supported	_____	Confident	_____	Positive	_____

Are you willing to schedule dedicated time to work on this goal daily? _____ If, so how much? _____

List five affirmations you will use to help you achieve this goal.

_____

_____

_____

_____

_____

Accept this goal as already true and write a thank you note to yourself for doing the work and to the universe/god for helping you achieve it.

_____

_____

_____

_____

_____

Describe any positive feelings/emotions you feel around this goal now.

_____

_____

_____

_____

Are you ready to take action towards this goal? _____

If not now, what will help you become ready?

_____

_____

_____

What does success look like?
Doodle, Notes, Images, Brainstorm, Mindmap

Visualize Success

Work

When will you begin working on this?_____

Have you added this goal to your vision board? _____ If not, when will you add it? _____

Where are you today compared to where you want to be with this goal? How can you get there?

Current Status	Goal	Difference/Actions Needed
_____	_____	_____
_____	_____	_____
_____	_____	_____
_____	_____	_____
_____	_____	_____

What skills and resources are already available to you and how can you use them?

Skills/Resources	How can you use it?
_____	_____
_____	_____
_____	_____
_____	_____

What skills and resources do you need and how might you acquire them?

Skills/Resources	How will you acquire it?
_____	_____
_____	_____
_____	_____
_____	_____
_____	_____

List any milestones along this journey.

How will you measure your successes and progress?

_____

How will you hold yourself accountable?

_____

What action will you take today? _____

What daily actions are required (habits)? Identify keystone habits.

Stop	Start	Continue	Increase	Limit

Action Plan

	Steps to Take/Checklist	Timeline
PHASE 1		Start Date:
PHASE 2		
PHASE 3		
PHASE 4		

30-Day Habit Tracker
Goal

Round 1		

Habit	Start Date	Day
1.		1 2 3 4 5 6 7 8 9 10 11 12 13 14 15 16 17 18 19 20 21 22 23 24 25 26 27 28 29 30
2.		1 2 3 4 5 6 7 8 9 10 11 12 13 14 15 16 17 18 19 20 21 22 23 24 25 26 27 28 29 30
3.		1 2 3 4 5 6 7 8 9 10 11 12 13 14 15 16 17 18 19 20 21 22 23 24 25 26 27 28 29 30
4.		1 2 3 4 5 6 7 8 9 10 11 12 13 14 15 16 17 18 19 20 21 22 23 24 25 26 27 28 29 30
5.		1 2 3 4 5 6 7 8 9 10 11 12 13 14 15 16 17 18 19 20 21 22 23 24 25 26 27 28 29 30

Round 2		

Habit	Start Date	Day
1.		1 2 3 4 5 6 7 8 9 10 11 12 13 14 15 16 17 18 19 20 21 22 23 24 25 26 27 28 29 30
2.		1 2 3 4 5 6 7 8 9 10 11 12 13 14 15 16 17 18 19 20 21 22 23 24 25 26 27 28 29 30
3.		1 2 3 4 5 6 7 8 9 10 11 12 13 14 15 16 17 18 19 20 21 22 23 24 25 26 27 28 29 30
4.		1 2 3 4 5 6 7 8 9 10 11 12 13 14 15 16 17 18 19 20 21 22 23 24 25 26 27 28 29 30
5.		1 2 3 4 5 6 7 8 9 10 11 12 13 14 15 16 17 18 19 20 21 22 23 24 25 26 27 28 29 30

Round 3		

Habit	Start Date	Day
1.		1 2 3 4 5 6 7 8 9 10 11 12 13 14 15 16 17 18 19 20 21 22 23 24 25 26 27 28 29 30
2.		1 2 3 4 5 6 7 8 9 10 11 12 13 14 15 16 17 18 19 20 21 22 23 24 25 26 27 28 29 30
3.		1 2 3 4 5 6 7 8 9 10 11 12 13 14 15 16 17 18 19 20 21 22 23 24 25 26 27 28 29 30
4.		1 2 3 4 5 6 7 8 9 10 11 12 13 14 15 16 17 18 19 20 21 22 23 24 25 26 27 28 29 30
5.		1 2 3 4 5 6 7 8 9 10 11 12 13 14 15 16 17 18 19 20 21 22 23 24 25 26 27 28 29 30

Round 4		

Habit	Start Date	Day
1.		1 2 3 4 5 6 7 8 9 10 11 12 13 14 15 16 17 18 19 20 21 22 23 24 25 26 27 28 29 30
2.		1 2 3 4 5 6 7 8 9 10 11 12 13 14 15 16 17 18 19 20 21 22 23 24 25 26 27 28 29 30
3.		1 2 3 4 5 6 7 8 9 10 11 12 13 14 15 16 17 18 19 20 21 22 23 24 25 26 27 28 29 30
4.		1 2 3 4 5 6 7 8 9 10 11 12 13 14 15 16 17 18 19 20 21 22 23 24 25 26 27 28 29 30
5.		1 2 3 4 5 6 7 8 9 10 11 12 13 14 15 16 17 18 19 20 21 22 23 24 25 26 27 28 29 30

Round 5		

Habit	Start Date	Day
1.		1 2 3 4 5 6 7 8 9 10 11 12 13 14 15 16 17 18 19 20 21 22 23 24 25 26 27 28 29 30
2.		1 2 3 4 5 6 7 8 9 10 11 12 13 14 15 16 17 18 19 20 21 22 23 24 25 26 27 28 29 30
3.		1 2 3 4 5 6 7 8 9 10 11 12 13 14 15 16 17 18 19 20 21 22 23 24 25 26 27 28 29 30
4.		1 2 3 4 5 6 7 8 9 10 11 12 13 14 15 16 17 18 19 20 21 22 23 24 25 26 27 28 29 30
5.		1 2 3 4 5 6 7 8 9 10 11 12 13 14 15 16 17 18 19 20 21 22 23 24 25 26 27 28 29 30

Round 6		

Habit	Start Date	Day
1.		1 2 3 4 5 6 7 8 9 10 11 12 13 14 15 16 17 18 19 20 21 22 23 24 25 26 27 28 29 30
2.		1 2 3 4 5 6 7 8 9 10 11 12 13 14 15 16 17 18 19 20 21 22 23 24 25 26 27 28 29 30
3.		1 2 3 4 5 6 7 8 9 10 11 12 13 14 15 16 17 18 19 20 21 22 23 24 25 26 27 28 29 30
4.		1 2 3 4 5 6 7 8 9 10 11 12 13 14 15 16 17 18 19 20 21 22 23 24 25 26 27 28 29 30
5.		1 2 3 4 5 6 7 8 9 10 11 12 13 14 15 16 17 18 19 20 21 22 23 24 25 26 27 28 29 30

Post-Work

Congratulations! You've achieved your goal. Now, celebrate your success. You deserve it!

After the celebration, it's time for evaluation. Take a look back on what you've experienced around this goal. Note any observations, obstacles, and lessons learned and how you apply them in the future.

Was the experience what you expected it to be? If not, why?_____

_____
_____
_____

What happened with this goal and its execution? Did anything stand out?

_____
_____
_____
_____
_____
_____

Did everything go as planned? _____   Did you stick to the timeline? _____
What went well?

_____
_____
_____
_____

What could've gone better?   How can you make adjustments in the future?

_____   _____
_____   _____
_____   _____
_____   _____

What lessons did you learn?   How will you apply them?

_____   _____
_____   _____
_____   _____
_____   _____

How have you grown from this experience?

_____
_____
_____

How will you maintain this success?

_____
_____
_____
_____

Goal # _____

Pre-Work

Specific	Measurable	Achievable	Realistic/Relevant	Time-bound

Use positive language to rewrite your finalized goal including the SMART elements from above.

_____

_____

What's your motivation? Why do you want to achieve this goal? (Also, do you want to achieve it for yourself or because someone else wants it for you?)

_____

_____

_____

_____

_____

This goals supports objectives: _____

Define this goal. Describe, *in vivid detail*, <u>exactly</u> what you want and what your success looks and feels likes. Use as many senses in the description as possible. Make, model, size, shape, color, year, location, etc.. See, hear, and feel. Use details, details, details!

_____

_____

_____

_____

_____

_____

_____

_____

_____

_____

_____

_____

_____

_____

_____

Success Checklist
Prework
Build SMART Goal
Understand Why
Develop Details
Identify Strengths & Weaknesses
Identify Support
Identify Reward
Assess Commitment
Identify Resources
Identify Changes
Develop Action Plan & Timeline
Work
Visualize & Plant the Seed
Take the 1st Step
Build Affirmation Cards
Track Habits for 30 Days
Execute Plan
Phase 1
Phase 2
Phase 3
Phase 4
Achieve Goal!
Postwork
Celebrate
Evaluate

Have you gotten a clear mental image of this goal? If not what additional details will bring greater clarity?

_____
_____
_____

Can you see yourself achieving this goal? _____

How will you know when you've achieved this goal?

_____
_____
_____
_____

Have you attempted this goal before? _____

What barriers have you encountered in the past and/or what obstacles can you anticipate? How will you overcome them?

Barriers/Obstacles/Fears   How will you overcome them?

_____   _____
_____   _____
_____   _____
_____   _____
_____   _____

What assets and advantages do you have?

Assets/Advantages   How can you use these?

_____   _____
_____   _____
_____   _____
_____   _____
_____   _____

Are there any feelings of pain or pleasure around this goal?

Pain/Pleasure   How can you use these emotions in your motivation?

_____   _____
_____   _____
_____   _____
_____   _____
_____   _____

How will you benefit from achieving this goal?

_____
_____
_____
_____

How might this achievement improve how you feel about yourself?

_____
_____
_____
_____

How will you reward yourself when you've achieved this goal?

_____
_____
_____
_____
_____

Who has already achieved this goal that you may be able to model? _____

Are you willing to research their process and adapt it to your needs? _____

Where else might you find assistance? _____

Who will support you in this process? _____

Rate the following on a scale from 1 – 10 (1 = low and 10 = high) to determine your readiness to achieve this goal and discover areas to work on.

Are you ………………

Committed	_____	Willing to sacrifice	_____	Willing to work now?	_____
Ready	_____	Disciplined	_____	Do you believe it?	_____
Deserving	_____	Consistent	_____	Focused	_____
Dedicated	_____	Capable	_____	Organized	_____
Supported	_____	Confident	_____	Positive	_____

Are you willing to schedule dedicated time to work on this goal daily? _____ If, so how much? _____

List five affirmations you will use to help you achieve this goal.

_____
_____
_____
_____
_____

Accept this goal as already true and write a thank you note to yourself for doing the work and to the universe/god for helping you achieve it.

_____
_____
_____
_____
_____

Describe any positive feelings/emotions you feel around this goal now.

_____
_____
_____
_____

Are you ready to take action towards this goal? _____

If not now, what will help you become ready?

_____
_____
_____

What does success look like?
Doodle, Notes, Images, Brainstorm, Mindmap

Visualize Success

Work

When will you begin working on this?_____

Have you added this goal to your vision board? _____ If not, when will you add it? _____

Where are you today compared to where you want to be with this goal? How can you get there?

Current Status	Goal	Difference/Actions Needed
_____	_____	_____
_____	_____	_____
_____	_____	_____
_____	_____	_____
_____	_____	_____

What skills and resources are already available to you and how can you use them?

Skills/Resources	How can you use it?
_____	_____
_____	_____
_____	_____
_____	_____

What skills and resources do you need and how might you acquire them?

Skills/Resources	How will you acquire it?
_____	_____
_____	_____
_____	_____
_____	_____
_____	_____

List any milestones along this journey.

How will you measure your successes and progress?

_____

_____

How will you hold yourself accountable?

_____

_____

What action will you take today? _____

What daily actions are required (habits)? Identify keystone habits.

Stop	Start	Continue	Increase	Limit

Action Plan

	Steps to Take/Checklist	Timeline
PHASE 1		Start Date:
PHASE 2		
PHASE 3		
PHASE 4		

30-Day Habit Tracker
Goal

Round 1

Habit	Start Date	Day																												
1.		1	2	3	4	5	6	7	8	9	10	11	12	13	14	15	16	17	18	19	20	21	22	23	24	25	26	27	28	29	30
2.		1	2	3	4	5	6	7	8	9	10	11	12	13	14	15	16	17	18	19	20	21	22	23	24	25	26	27	28	29	30
3.		1	2	3	4	5	6	7	8	9	10	11	12	13	14	15	16	17	18	19	20	21	22	23	24	25	26	27	28	29	30
4.		1	2	3	4	5	6	7	8	9	10	11	12	13	14	15	16	17	18	19	20	21	22	23	24	25	26	27	28	29	30
5.		1	2	3	4	5	6	7	8	9	10	11	12	13	14	15	16	17	18	19	20	21	22	23	24	25	26	27	28	29	30

Round 2

Habit	Start Date	Day																												
1.		1	2	3	4	5	6	7	8	9	10	11	12	13	14	15	16	17	18	19	20	21	22	23	24	25	26	27	28	29	30
2.		1	2	3	4	5	6	7	8	9	10	11	12	13	14	15	16	17	18	19	20	21	22	23	24	25	26	27	28	29	30
3.		1	2	3	4	5	6	7	8	9	10	11	12	13	14	15	16	17	18	19	20	21	22	23	24	25	26	27	28	29	30
4.		1	2	3	4	5	6	7	8	9	10	11	12	13	14	15	16	17	18	19	20	21	22	23	24	25	26	27	28	29	30
5.		1	2	3	4	5	6	7	8	9	10	11	12	13	14	15	16	17	18	19	20	21	22	23	24	25	26	27	28	29	30

Round 3

Habit	Start Date	Day																												
1.		1	2	3	4	5	6	7	8	9	10	11	12	13	14	15	16	17	18	19	20	21	22	23	24	25	26	27	28	29	30
2.		1	2	3	4	5	6	7	8	9	10	11	12	13	14	15	16	17	18	19	20	21	22	23	24	25	26	27	28	29	30
3.		1	2	3	4	5	6	7	8	9	10	11	12	13	14	15	16	17	18	19	20	21	22	23	24	25	26	27	28	29	30
4.		1	2	3	4	5	6	7	8	9	10	11	12	13	14	15	16	17	18	19	20	21	22	23	24	25	26	27	28	29	30
5.		1	2	3	4	5	6	7	8	9	10	11	12	13	14	15	16	17	18	19	20	21	22	23	24	25	26	27	28	29	30

Round 4

Habit	Start Date	Day																												
1.		1	2	3	4	5	6	7	8	9	10	11	12	13	14	15	16	17	18	19	20	21	22	23	24	25	26	27	28	29	30
2.		1	2	3	4	5	6	7	8	9	10	11	12	13	14	15	16	17	18	19	20	21	22	23	24	25	26	27	28	29	30
3.		1	2	3	4	5	6	7	8	9	10	11	12	13	14	15	16	17	18	19	20	21	22	23	24	25	26	27	28	29	30
4.		1	2	3	4	5	6	7	8	9	10	11	12	13	14	15	16	17	18	19	20	21	22	23	24	25	26	27	28	29	30
5.		1	2	3	4	5	6	7	8	9	10	11	12	13	14	15	16	17	18	19	20	21	22	23	24	25	26	27	28	29	30

Round 5

Habit	Start Date	Day																												
1.		1	2	3	4	5	6	7	8	9	10	11	12	13	14	15	16	17	18	19	20	21	22	23	24	25	26	27	28	29	30
2.		1	2	3	4	5	6	7	8	9	10	11	12	13	14	15	16	17	18	19	20	21	22	23	24	25	26	27	28	29	30
3.		1	2	3	4	5	6	7	8	9	10	11	12	13	14	15	16	17	18	19	20	21	22	23	24	25	26	27	28	29	30
4.		1	2	3	4	5	6	7	8	9	10	11	12	13	14	15	16	17	18	19	20	21	22	23	24	25	26	27	28	29	30
5.		1	2	3	4	5	6	7	8	9	10	11	12	13	14	15	16	17	18	19	20	21	22	23	24	25	26	27	28	29	30

Round 6

Habit	Start Date	Day																												
1.		1	2	3	4	5	6	7	8	9	10	11	12	13	14	15	16	17	18	19	20	21	22	23	24	25	26	27	28	29	30
2.		1	2	3	4	5	6	7	8	9	10	11	12	13	14	15	16	17	18	19	20	21	22	23	24	25	26	27	28	29	30
3.		1	2	3	4	5	6	7	8	9	10	11	12	13	14	15	16	17	18	19	20	21	22	23	24	25	26	27	28	29	30
4.		1	2	3	4	5	6	7	8	9	10	11	12	13	14	15	16	17	18	19	20	21	22	23	24	25	26	27	28	29	30
5.		1	2	3	4	5	6	7	8	9	10	11	12	13	14	15	16	17	18	19	20	21	22	23	24	25	26	27	28	29	30

Post-Work

Congratulations! You've achieved your goal. Now, celebrate your success. You deserve it!

After the celebration, it's time for evaluation. Take a look back on what you've experienced around this goal. Note any observations, obstacles, and lessons learned and how you apply them in the future.

Was the experience what you expected it to be? If not, why?_____

_____
_____
_____

 What happened with this goal and its execution? Did anything stand out?

_____
_____
_____
_____
_____
_____

Did everything go as planned? _____   Did you stick to the timeline? _____
What went well?

_____
_____
_____
_____

What could've gone better?   How can you make adjustments in the future?

_____   _____
_____   _____
_____   _____
_____   _____

What lessons did you learn?   How will you apply them?

_____   _____
_____   _____
_____   _____
_____   _____

How have you grown from this experience?

_____
_____
_____
_____

How will you maintain this success?

_____
_____
_____
_____

Goal # _____

Pre-Work

Specific	Measurable	Achievable	Realistic/Relevant	Time-bound

Use positive language to rewrite your finalized goal including the SMART elements from above.

_____

_____

What's your motivation? Why do you want to achieve this goal? (Also, do you want to achieve it for yourself or because someone else wants it for you?)

_____

_____

_____

_____

This goals supports objectives: _____

Define this goal. Describe, *in vivid detail*, exactly what you want and what your success looks and feels likes. Use as many senses in the description as possible. Make, model, size, shape, color, year, location, etc.. See, hear, and feel. Use details, details, details!

_____

_____

_____

_____

_____

_____

_____

_____

_____

_____

_____

_____

_____

_____

_____

Success Checklist
Prework
Build SMART Goal
Understand Why
Develop Details
Identify Strengths & Weaknesses
Identify Support
Identify Reward
Assess Commitment
Identify Resources
Identify Changes
Develop Action Plan & Timeline
Work
Visualize & Plant the Seed
Take the 1st Step
Build Affirmation Cards
Track Habits for 30 Days
Execute Plan
Phase 1
Phase 2
Phase 3
Phase 4
Achieve Goal!
Postwork
Celebrate
Evaluate

Have you gotten a clear mental image of this goal? If not what additional details will bring greater clarity?

_____
_____
_____

Can you see yourself achieving this goal? _____

How will you know when you've achieved this goal?

_____
_____
_____
_____

Have you attempted this goal before? _____

What barriers have you encountered in the past and/or what obstacles can you anticipate? How will you overcome them?

Barriers/Obstacles/Fears	How will you overcome them?
_____	_____
_____	_____
_____	_____
_____	_____
_____	_____

What assets and advantages do you have?

Assets/Advantages	How can you use these?
_____	_____
_____	_____
_____	_____
_____	_____
_____	_____

Are there any feelings of pain or pleasure around this goal?

Pain/Pleasure	How can you use these emotions in your motivation?
_____	_____
_____	_____
_____	_____
_____	_____
_____	_____

How will you benefit from achieving this goal?

_____
_____
_____
_____

How might this achievement improve how you feel about yourself?

_____
_____
_____
_____

How will you reward yourself when you've achieved this goal?

_____

_____

_____

_____

_____

Who has already achieved this goal that you may be able to model? _____

Are you willing to research their process and adapt it to your needs? _____

Where else might you find assistance? _____

Who will support you in this process? _____

Rate the following on a scale from 1 – 10 (1 = low and 10 = high) to determine your readiness to achieve this goal and discover areas to work on.

Are you ………………..

Committed	_____	Willing to sacrifice	_____	Willing to work now?	_____
Ready	_____	Disciplined	_____	Do you believe it?	_____
Deserving	_____	Consistent	_____	Focused	_____
Dedicated	_____	Capable	_____	Organized	_____
Supported	_____	Confident	_____	Positive	_____

Are you willing to schedule dedicated time to work on this goal daily? _____ If, so how much? _____

List five affirmations you will use to help you achieve this goal.

_____

_____

_____

_____

_____

Accept this goal as already true and write a thank you note to yourself for doing the work and to the universe/god for helping you achieve it.

_____

_____

_____

_____

_____

Describe any positive feelings/emotions you feel around this goal now.

_____

_____

_____

_____

Are you ready to take action towards this goal? _____

If not now, what will help you become ready?

_____

_____

_____

What does success look like?
Doodle, Notes, Images, Brainstorm, Mindmap

Work

When will you begin working on this?_____

Have you added this goal to your vision board? _____ If not, when will you add it? _____

Where are you today compared to where you want to be with this goal? How can you get there?

Current Status	Goal	Difference/Actions Needed
_____	_____	_____
_____	_____	_____
_____	_____	_____
_____	_____	_____
_____	_____	_____

What skills and resources are already available to you and how can you use them?

Skills/Resources	How can you use it?
_____	_____
_____	_____
_____	_____
_____	_____

What skills and resources do you need and how might you acquire them?

Skills/Resources	How will you acquire it?
_____	_____
_____	_____
_____	_____
_____	_____
_____	_____

List any milestones along this journey.

How will you measure your successes and progress?

_____

_____

How will you hold yourself accountable?

_____

_____

What action will you take today? _____

What daily actions are required (habits)? Identify keystone habits.

Stop	Start	Continue	Increase	Limit

Action Plan

	Steps to Take/Checklist	Timeline
PHASE 1		Start Date:
PHASE 2		
PHASE 3		
PHASE 4		

30-Day Habit Tracker
Goal

Round 1																															

Habit	Start Date	Day
1.		1 2 3 4 5 6 7 8 9 10 11 12 13 14 15 16 17 18 19 20 21 22 23 24 25 26 27 28 29 30
2.		1 2 3 4 5 6 7 8 9 10 11 12 13 14 15 16 17 18 19 20 21 22 23 24 25 26 27 28 29 30
3.		1 2 3 4 5 6 7 8 9 10 11 12 13 14 15 16 17 18 19 20 21 22 23 24 25 26 27 28 29 30
4.		1 2 3 4 5 6 7 8 9 10 11 12 13 14 15 16 17 18 19 20 21 22 23 24 25 26 27 28 29 30
5.		1 2 3 4 5 6 7 8 9 10 11 12 13 14 15 16 17 18 19 20 21 22 23 24 25 26 27 28 29 30

Round 2

Habit	Start Date	Day
1.		1 2 3 4 5 6 7 8 9 10 11 12 13 14 15 16 17 18 19 20 21 22 23 24 25 26 27 28 29 30
2.		1 2 3 4 5 6 7 8 9 10 11 12 13 14 15 16 17 18 19 20 21 22 23 24 25 26 27 28 29 30
3.		1 2 3 4 5 6 7 8 9 10 11 12 13 14 15 16 17 18 19 20 21 22 23 24 25 26 27 28 29 30
4.		1 2 3 4 5 6 7 8 9 10 11 12 13 14 15 16 17 18 19 20 21 22 23 24 25 26 27 28 29 30
5.		1 2 3 4 5 6 7 8 9 10 11 12 13 14 15 16 17 18 19 20 21 22 23 24 25 26 27 28 29 30

Round 3

Habit	Start Date	Day
1.		1 2 3 4 5 6 7 8 9 10 11 12 13 14 15 16 17 18 19 20 21 22 23 24 25 26 27 28 29 30
2.		1 2 3 4 5 6 7 8 9 10 11 12 13 14 15 16 17 18 19 20 21 22 23 24 25 26 27 28 29 30
3.		1 2 3 4 5 6 7 8 9 10 11 12 13 14 15 16 17 18 19 20 21 22 23 24 25 26 27 28 29 30
4.		1 2 3 4 5 6 7 8 9 10 11 12 13 14 15 16 17 18 19 20 21 22 23 24 25 26 27 28 29 30
5.		1 2 3 4 5 6 7 8 9 10 11 12 13 14 15 16 17 18 19 20 21 22 23 24 25 26 27 28 29 30

Round 4

Habit	Start Date	Day
1.		1 2 3 4 5 6 7 8 9 10 11 12 13 14 15 16 17 18 19 20 21 22 23 24 25 26 27 28 29 30
2.		1 2 3 4 5 6 7 8 9 10 11 12 13 14 15 16 17 18 19 20 21 22 23 24 25 26 27 28 29 30
3.		1 2 3 4 5 6 7 8 9 10 11 12 13 14 15 16 17 18 19 20 21 22 23 24 25 26 27 28 29 30
4.		1 2 3 4 5 6 7 8 9 10 11 12 13 14 15 16 17 18 19 20 21 22 23 24 25 26 27 28 29 30
5.		1 2 3 4 5 6 7 8 9 10 11 12 13 14 15 16 17 18 19 20 21 22 23 24 25 26 27 28 29 30

Round 5

Habit	Start Date	Day
1.		1 2 3 4 5 6 7 8 9 10 11 12 13 14 15 16 17 18 19 20 21 22 23 24 25 26 27 28 29 30
2.		1 2 3 4 5 6 7 8 9 10 11 12 13 14 15 16 17 18 19 20 21 22 23 24 25 26 27 28 29 30
3.		1 2 3 4 5 6 7 8 9 10 11 12 13 14 15 16 17 18 19 20 21 22 23 24 25 26 27 28 29 30
4.		1 2 3 4 5 6 7 8 9 10 11 12 13 14 15 16 17 18 19 20 21 22 23 24 25 26 27 28 29 30
5.		1 2 3 4 5 6 7 8 9 10 11 12 13 14 15 16 17 18 19 20 21 22 23 24 25 26 27 28 29 30

Round 6

Habit	Start Date	Day
1.		1 2 3 4 5 6 7 8 9 10 11 12 13 14 15 16 17 18 19 20 21 22 23 24 25 26 27 28 29 30
2.		1 2 3 4 5 6 7 8 9 10 11 12 13 14 15 16 17 18 19 20 21 22 23 24 25 26 27 28 29 30
3.		1 2 3 4 5 6 7 8 9 10 11 12 13 14 15 16 17 18 19 20 21 22 23 24 25 26 27 28 29 30
4.		1 2 3 4 5 6 7 8 9 10 11 12 13 14 15 16 17 18 19 20 21 22 23 24 25 26 27 28 29 30
5.		1 2 3 4 5 6 7 8 9 10 11 12 13 14 15 16 17 18 19 20 21 22 23 24 25 26 27 28 29 30

Post-Work

Congratulations! You've achieved your goal. Now, celebrate your success. You deserve it!

After the celebration, it's time for evaluation. Take a look back on what you've experienced around this goal. Note any observations, obstacles, and lessons learned and how you apply them in the future.

Was the experience what you expected it to be? If not, why?_____

_____
_____
_____

 What happened with this goal and its execution? Did anything stand out?

_____
_____
_____
_____
_____
_____

Did everything go as planned? _____   Did you stick to the timeline? _____

What went well?

_____
_____
_____
_____

What could've gone better?   How can you make adjustments in the future?

_____   _____
_____   _____
_____   _____
_____   _____

What lessons did you learn?   How will you apply them?

_____   _____
_____   _____
_____   _____
_____   _____

How have you grown from this experience?

_____
_____
_____
_____

How will you maintain this success?

_____
_____
_____
_____

Goal # _____

Pre-Work

Specific	Measurable	Achievable	Realistic/Relevant	Time-bound

Use positive language to rewrite your finalized goal including the SMART elements from above.

_____

_____

What's your motivation? Why do you want to achieve this goal? (Also, do you want to achieve it for yourself or because someone else wants it for you?)

_____

_____

_____

_____

_____

This goals supports objectives: _____

Define this goal. Describe, *in vivid detail*, <u>exactly</u> what you want and what your success looks and feels likes. Use as many senses in the description as possible. Make, model, size, shape, color, year, location, etc.. See, hear, and feel. Use details, details, details!

_____

_____

_____

_____

_____

_____

_____

_____

_____

_____

_____

_____

_____

_____

_____

_____

Success Checklist
Prework
Build SMART Goal
Understand Why
Develop Details
Identify Strengths & Weaknesses
Identify Support
Identify Reward
Assess Commitment
Identify Resources
Identify Changes
Develop Action Plan & Timeline
Work
Visualize & Plant the Seed
Take the 1st Step
Build Affirmation Cards
Track Habits for 30 Days
Execute Plan
Phase 1
Phase 2
Phase 3
Phase 4
Achieve Goal!
Postwork
Celebrate
Evaluate

Have you gotten a clear mental image of this goal? If not what additional details will bring greater clarity?

_____

_____

_____

Can you see yourself achieving this goal? _____

How will you know when you've achieved this goal?

_____

_____

_____

_____

Have you attempted this goal before? _____

What barriers have you encountered in the past and/or what obstacles can you anticipate? How will you overcome them?

Barriers/Obstacles/Fears	How will you overcome them?
_____	_____
_____	_____
_____	_____
_____	_____
_____	_____

What assets and advantages do you have?

Assets/Advantages	How can you use these?
_____	_____
_____	_____
_____	_____
_____	_____
_____	_____

Are there any feelings of pain or pleasure around this goal?

Pain/Pleasure	How can you use these emotions in your motivation?
_____	_____
_____	_____
_____	_____
_____	_____
_____	_____

How will you benefit from achieving this goal?

_____

_____

_____

_____

How might this achievement improve how you feel about yourself?

_____

_____

_____

_____

How will you reward yourself when you've achieved this goal?

_____

_____

_____

_____

_____

Who has already achieved this goal that you may be able to model? _____

Are you willing to research their process and adapt it to your needs? _____

Where else might you find assistance? _____

Who will support you in this process? _____

Rate the following on a scale from 1 – 10 (1 = low and 10 = high) to determine your readiness to achieve this goal and discover areas to work on.

Are you ………………

Committed	_____	Willing to sacrifice	_____	Willing to work now?	_____
Ready	_____	Disciplined	_____	Do you believe it?	_____
Deserving	_____	Consistent	_____	Focused	_____
Dedicated	_____	Capable	_____	Organized	_____
Supported	_____	Confident	_____	Positive	_____

Are you willing to schedule dedicated time to work on this goal daily? _____ If, so how much? _____

List five affirmations you will use to help you achieve this goal.

_____

_____

_____

_____

_____

Accept this goal as already true and write a thank you note to yourself for doing the work and to the universe/god for helping you achieve it.

_____

_____

_____

_____

_____

Describe any positive feelings/emotions you feel around this goal now.

_____

_____

_____

_____

Are you ready to take action towards this goal? _____

If not now, what will help you become ready?

_____

_____

_____

What does success look like?
Doodle, Notes, Images, Brainstorm, Mindmap

Visualize Success

Work

When will you begin working on this?_____

Have you added this goal to your vision board? _____ If not, when will you add it? _____

Where are you today compared to where you want to be with this goal? How can you get there?

Current Status	Goal	Difference/Actions Needed
_____	_____	_____
_____	_____	_____
_____	_____	_____
_____	_____	_____
_____	_____	_____

What skills and resources are already available to you and how can you use them?

Skills/Resources   How can you use it?

_____   _____

_____   _____

_____   _____

_____   _____

What skills and resources do you need and how might you acquire them?

Skills/Resources   How will you acquire it?

_____   _____

_____   _____

_____   _____

_____   _____

_____   _____

List any milestones along this journey.   How will you measure your successes and progress?

_____   _____

_____   How will you hold yourself accountable?

_____   _____

_____   _____

_____   _____

What action will you take today? _____

What daily actions are required (habits)? Identify keystone habits.

Stop	Start	Continue	Increase	Limit

Action Plan

	Steps to Take/Checklist	Timeline
PHASE 1		Start Date:
PHASE 2		
PHASE 3		
PHASE 4		

30-Day Habit Tracker
Goal

Round 1				

Habit	Start Date	Day																													
1.		1	2	3	4	5	6	7	8	9	10	11	12	13	14	15	16	17	18	19	20	21	22	23	24	25	26	27	28	29	30
2.		1	2	3	4	5	6	7	8	9	10	11	12	13	14	15	16	17	18	19	20	21	22	23	24	25	26	27	28	29	30
3.		1	2	3	4	5	6	7	8	9	10	11	12	13	14	15	16	17	18	19	20	21	22	23	24	25	26	27	28	29	30
4.		1	2	3	4	5	6	7	8	9	10	11	12	13	14	15	16	17	18	19	20	21	22	23	24	25	26	27	28	29	30
5.		1	2	3	4	5	6	7	8	9	10	11	12	13	14	15	16	17	18	19	20	21	22	23	24	25	26	27	28	29	30

Round 2				

Habit	Start Date	Day																													
1.		1	2	3	4	5	6	7	8	9	10	11	12	13	14	15	16	17	18	19	20	21	22	23	24	25	26	27	28	29	30
2.		1	2	3	4	5	6	7	8	9	10	11	12	13	14	15	16	17	18	19	20	21	22	23	24	25	26	27	28	29	30
3.		1	2	3	4	5	6	7	8	9	10	11	12	13	14	15	16	17	18	19	20	21	22	23	24	25	26	27	28	29	30
4.		1	2	3	4	5	6	7	8	9	10	11	12	13	14	15	16	17	18	19	20	21	22	23	24	25	26	27	28	29	30
5.		1	2	3	4	5	6	7	8	9	10	11	12	13	14	15	16	17	18	19	20	21	22	23	24	25	26	27	28	29	30

Round 3				

Habit	Start Date	Day																													
1.		1	2	3	4	5	6	7	8	9	10	11	12	13	14	15	16	17	18	19	20	21	22	23	24	25	26	27	28	29	30
2.		1	2	3	4	5	6	7	8	9	10	11	12	13	14	15	16	17	18	19	20	21	22	23	24	25	26	27	28	29	30
3.		1	2	3	4	5	6	7	8	9	10	11	12	13	14	15	16	17	18	19	20	21	22	23	24	25	26	27	28	29	30
4.		1	2	3	4	5	6	7	8	9	10	11	12	13	14	15	16	17	18	19	20	21	22	23	24	25	26	27	28	29	30
5.		1	2	3	4	5	6	7	8	9	10	11	12	13	14	15	16	17	18	19	20	21	22	23	24	25	26	27	28	29	30

Round 4				

Habit	Start Date	Day																													
1.		1	2	3	4	5	6	7	8	9	10	11	12	13	14	15	16	17	18	19	20	21	22	23	24	25	26	27	28	29	30
2.		1	2	3	4	5	6	7	8	9	10	11	12	13	14	15	16	17	18	19	20	21	22	23	24	25	26	27	28	29	30
3.		1	2	3	4	5	6	7	8	9	10	11	12	13	14	15	16	17	18	19	20	21	22	23	24	25	26	27	28	29	30
4.		1	2	3	4	5	6	7	8	9	10	11	12	13	14	15	16	17	18	19	20	21	22	23	24	25	26	27	28	29	30
5.		1	2	3	4	5	6	7	8	9	10	11	12	13	14	15	16	17	18	19	20	21	22	23	24	25	26	27	28	29	30

Round 5				

Habit	Start Date	Day																													
1.		1	2	3	4	5	6	7	8	9	10	11	12	13	14	15	16	17	18	19	20	21	22	23	24	25	26	27	28	29	30
2.		1	2	3	4	5	6	7	8	9	10	11	12	13	14	15	16	17	18	19	20	21	22	23	24	25	26	27	28	29	30
3.		1	2	3	4	5	6	7	8	9	10	11	12	13	14	15	16	17	18	19	20	21	22	23	24	25	26	27	28	29	30
4.		1	2	3	4	5	6	7	8	9	10	11	12	13	14	15	16	17	18	19	20	21	22	23	24	25	26	27	28	29	30
5.		1	2	3	4	5	6	7	8	9	10	11	12	13	14	15	16	17	18	19	20	21	22	23	24	25	26	27	28	29	30

Round 6				

Habit	Start Date	Day																													
1.		1	2	3	4	5	6	7	8	9	10	11	12	13	14	15	16	17	18	19	20	21	22	23	24	25	26	27	28	29	30
2.		1	2	3	4	5	6	7	8	9	10	11	12	13	14	15	16	17	18	19	20	21	22	23	24	25	26	27	28	29	30
3.		1	2	3	4	5	6	7	8	9	10	11	12	13	14	15	16	17	18	19	20	21	22	23	24	25	26	27	28	29	30
4.		1	2	3	4	5	6	7	8	9	10	11	12	13	14	15	16	17	18	19	20	21	22	23	24	25	26	27	28	29	30
5.		1	2	3	4	5	6	7	8	9	10	11	12	13	14	15	16	17	18	19	20	21	22	23	24	25	26	27	28	29	30

Post-Work

Congratulations! You've achieved your goal. Now, celebrate your success. You deserve it!

After the celebration, it's time for evaluation. Take a look back on what you've experienced around this goal. Note any observations, obstacles, and lessons learned and how you apply them in the future.

Was the experience what you expected it to be? If not, why?_____

_____
_____
_____

What happened with this goal and its execution? Did anything stand out?

_____
_____
_____
_____
_____
_____

Did everything go as planned? _____   Did you stick to the timeline? _____
What went well?

_____
_____
_____
_____

What could've gone better?   How can you make adjustments in the future?

_____   _____
_____   _____
_____   _____
_____   _____

What lessons did you learn?   How will you apply them?

_____   _____
_____   _____
_____   _____
_____   _____

How have you grown from this experience?

_____
_____
_____
_____

How will you maintain this success?

_____
_____
_____
_____

Goal # _____

☐ _____
Date Completed

Pre-Work

Specific	Measurable	Achievable	Realistic/Relevant	Time-bound

Use positive language to rewrite your finalized goal including the SMART elements from above.

_____

_____

What's your motivation? Why do you want to achieve this goal? (Also, do you want to achieve it for yourself or because someone else wants it for you?)

_____

_____

_____

_____

_____

This goals supports objectives: _____

Define this goal. Describe, *in vivid detail*, <u>exactly</u> what you want and what your success looks and feels likes. Use as many senses in the description as possible. Make, model, size, shape, color, year, location, etc.. See, hear, and feel. Use details, details, details!

Success Checklist
Prework
Build SMART Goal
Understand Why
Develop Details
Identify Strengths & Weaknesses
Identify Support
Identify Reward
Assess Commitment
Identify Resources
Identify Changes
Develop Action Plan & Timeline
Work
Visualize & Plant the Seed
Take the 1st Step
Build Affirmation Cards
Track Habits for 30 Days
Execute Plan
Phase 1
Phase 2
Phase 3
Phase 4
Achieve Goal!
Postwork
Celebrate
Evaluate

Have you gotten a clear mental image of this goal? If not what additional details will bring greater clarity?

_____

_____

_____

Can you see yourself achieving this goal? _____

How will you know when you've achieved this goal?

_____

_____

_____

_____

Have you attempted this goal before? _____

What barriers have you encountered in the past and/or what obstacles can you anticipate? How will you overcome them?

Barriers/Obstacles/Fears	How will you overcome them?
_____	_____
_____	_____
_____	_____
_____	_____
_____	_____

What assets and advantages do you have?

Assets/Advantages	How can you use these?
_____	_____
_____	_____
_____	_____
_____	_____
_____	_____

Are there any feelings of pain or pleasure around this goal?

Pain/Pleasure	How can you use these emotions in your motivation?
_____	_____
_____	_____
_____	_____
_____	_____
_____	_____

How will you benefit from achieving this goal?

_____

_____

_____

_____

How might this achievement improve how you feel about yourself?

_____

_____

_____

_____

How will you reward yourself when you've achieved this goal?

_____

_____

_____

_____

_____

Who has already achieved this goal that you may be able to model? _____

Are you willing to research their process and adapt it to your needs? _____

Where else might you find assistance? _____

Who will support you in this process? _____

Rate the following on a scale from 1 – 10 (1 = low and 10 = high) to determine your readiness to achieve this goal and discover areas to work on.

Are you ………………

Committed	_____	Willing to sacrifice	_____	Willing to work now?	_____
Ready	_____	Disciplined	_____	Do you believe it?	_____
Deserving	_____	Consistent	_____	Focused	_____
Dedicated	_____	Capable	_____	Organized	_____
Supported	_____	Confident	_____	Positive	_____

Are you willing to schedule dedicated time to work on this goal daily? _____ If, so how much? _____

List five affirmations you will use to help you achieve this goal.

_____

_____

_____

_____

_____

Accept this goal as already true and write a thank you note to yourself for doing the work and to the universe/god for helping you achieve it.

_____

_____

_____

_____

_____

Describe any positive feelings/emotions you feel around this goal now.

_____

_____

_____

_____

Are you ready to take action towards this goal? _____

If not now, what will help you become ready?

_____

_____

_____

What does success look like?
Doodle, Notes, Images, Brainstorm, Mindmap

Visualize Success

Work

When will you begin working on this?_____

Have you added this goal to your vision board? _____ If not, when will you add it? _____

Where are you today compared to where you want to be with this goal? How can you get there?

Current Status	Goal	Difference/Actions Needed
_____	_____	_____
_____	_____	_____
_____	_____	_____
_____	_____	_____
_____	_____	_____

What skills and resources are already available to you and how can you use them?

Skills/Resources   How can you use it?

_____   _____

_____   _____

_____   _____

_____   _____

What skills and resources do you need and how might you acquire them?

Skills/Resources   How will you acquire it?

_____   _____

_____   _____

_____   _____

_____   _____

_____   _____

List any milestones along this journey.   How will you measure your successes and progress?

_____   _____

_____   How will you hold yourself accountable?

_____   _____

_____   _____

What action will you take today? _____

What daily actions are required (habits)? Identify keystone habits.

Stop	Start	Continue	Increase	Limit

Action Plan

	Steps to Take/Checklist	Timeline
PHASE 1		**Start Date:**
PHASE 2		
PHASE 3		
PHASE 4		

30-Day Habit Tracker
Goal

Round 1																																	
Habit	Start Date	Day																													
1.		1	2	3	4	5	6	7	8	9	10	11	12	13	14	15	16	17	18	19	20	21	22	23	24	25	26	27	28	29	30
2.		1	2	3	4	5	6	7	8	9	10	11	12	13	14	15	16	17	18	19	20	21	22	23	24	25	26	27	28	29	30
3.		1	2	3	4	5	6	7	8	9	10	11	12	13	14	15	16	17	18	19	20	21	22	23	24	25	26	27	28	29	30
4.		1	2	3	4	5	6	7	8	9	10	11	12	13	14	15	16	17	18	19	20	21	22	23	24	25	26	27	28	29	30
5.		1	2	3	4	5	6	7	8	9	10	11	12	13	14	15	16	17	18	19	20	21	22	23	24	25	26	27	28	29	30

Round 2																																	
Habit	Start Date	Day																													
1.		1	2	3	4	5	6	7	8	9	10	11	12	13	14	15	16	17	18	19	20	21	22	23	24	25	26	27	28	29	30
2.		1	2	3	4	5	6	7	8	9	10	11	12	13	14	15	16	17	18	19	20	21	22	23	24	25	26	27	28	29	30
3.		1	2	3	4	5	6	7	8	9	10	11	12	13	14	15	16	17	18	19	20	21	22	23	24	25	26	27	28	29	30
4.		1	2	3	4	5	6	7	8	9	10	11	12	13	14	15	16	17	18	19	20	21	22	23	24	25	26	27	28	29	30
5.		1	2	3	4	5	6	7	8	9	10	11	12	13	14	15	16	17	18	19	20	21	22	23	24	25	26	27	28	29	30

Round 3																																	
Habit	Start Date	Day																													
1.		1	2	3	4	5	6	7	8	9	10	11	12	13	14	15	16	17	18	19	20	21	22	23	24	25	26	27	28	29	30
2.		1	2	3	4	5	6	7	8	9	10	11	12	13	14	15	16	17	18	19	20	21	22	23	24	25	26	27	28	29	30
3.		1	2	3	4	5	6	7	8	9	10	11	12	13	14	15	16	17	18	19	20	21	22	23	24	25	26	27	28	29	30
4.		1	2	3	4	5	6	7	8	9	10	11	12	13	14	15	16	17	18	19	20	21	22	23	24	25	26	27	28	29	30
5.		1	2	3	4	5	6	7	8	9	10	11	12	13	14	15	16	17	18	19	20	21	22	23	24	25	26	27	28	29	30

Round 4																																	
Habit	Start Date	Day																													
1.		1	2	3	4	5	6	7	8	9	10	11	12	13	14	15	16	17	18	19	20	21	22	23	24	25	26	27	28	29	30
2.		1	2	3	4	5	6	7	8	9	10	11	12	13	14	15	16	17	18	19	20	21	22	23	24	25	26	27	28	29	30
3.		1	2	3	4	5	6	7	8	9	10	11	12	13	14	15	16	17	18	19	20	21	22	23	24	25	26	27	28	29	30
4.		1	2	3	4	5	6	7	8	9	10	11	12	13	14	15	16	17	18	19	20	21	22	23	24	25	26	27	28	29	30
5.		1	2	3	4	5	6	7	8	9	10	11	12	13	14	15	16	17	18	19	20	21	22	23	24	25	26	27	28	29	30

Round 5																																	
Habit	Start Date	Day																													
1.		1	2	3	4	5	6	7	8	9	10	11	12	13	14	15	16	17	18	19	20	21	22	23	24	25	26	27	28	29	30
2.		1	2	3	4	5	6	7	8	9	10	11	12	13	14	15	16	17	18	19	20	21	22	23	24	25	26	27	28	29	30
3.		1	2	3	4	5	6	7	8	9	10	11	12	13	14	15	16	17	18	19	20	21	22	23	24	25	26	27	28	29	30
4.		1	2	3	4	5	6	7	8	9	10	11	12	13	14	15	16	17	18	19	20	21	22	23	24	25	26	27	28	29	30
5.		1	2	3	4	5	6	7	8	9	10	11	12	13	14	15	16	17	18	19	20	21	22	23	24	25	26	27	28	29	30

Round 6																																	
Habit	Start Date	Day																													
1.		1	2	3	4	5	6	7	8	9	10	11	12	13	14	15	16	17	18	19	20	21	22	23	24	25	26	27	28	29	30
2.		1	2	3	4	5	6	7	8	9	10	11	12	13	14	15	16	17	18	19	20	21	22	23	24	25	26	27	28	29	30
3.		1	2	3	4	5	6	7	8	9	10	11	12	13	14	15	16	17	18	19	20	21	22	23	24	25	26	27	28	29	30
4.		1	2	3	4	5	6	7	8	9	10	11	12	13	14	15	16	17	18	19	20	21	22	23	24	25	26	27	28	29	30
5.		1	2	3	4	5	6	7	8	9	10	11	12	13	14	15	16	17	18	19	20	21	22	23	24	25	26	27	28	29	30

Post-Work

Congratulations! You've achieved your goal. Now, celebrate your success. You deserve it!

After the celebration, it's time for evaluation. Take a look back on what you've experienced around this goal. Note any observations, obstacles, and lessons learned and how you apply them in the future.

Was the experience what you expected it to be? If not, why?_____

_____
_____
_____

What happened with this goal and its execution? Did anything stand out?

_____
_____
_____
_____
_____
_____

Did everything go as planned? _____   Did you stick to the timeline? _____

What went well?

_____
_____
_____
_____

What could've gone better?   How can you make adjustments in the future?

_____   _____
_____   _____
_____   _____
_____   _____

What lessons did you learn?   How will you apply them?

_____   _____
_____   _____
_____   _____
_____   _____

How have you grown from this experience?

_____
_____
_____
_____

How will you maintain this success?

_____
_____
_____
_____